Walking the Heath – an introduction

A guided tour of over 1,000 years of recorded

London's most attractive and important open spaces

by

Neil Rhind MBE FSA
Vice-President of the Blackheath Society

Dr Roger Marshall MA PhD
Committee member of the Blackheath Society

Published by the Blackheath Society

Third impression 2021

Contents

1. The West Walk

2. The East Walk

3. The Central Walk

Introduction

By Howard Shields
Chairman of the Blackheath Society

This booklet is published by the Blackheath Society as a guide for Heath walkers wishing to know a little more about what there is to see. As you will know from this publication, we are extremely fortunate that, thanks principally to the hard work of **Neil Rhind**, a great deal is known about its history. It can be judged as a companion booklet to our highly popular *Blackheath Village Trail and Guide* first published by the Society in 2005 and subsequently reprinted.

The Blackheath Society exists to preserve and enhance Blackheath and, specifically, to protect the Heath from encroachment or disfigurement. The Heath remains inviolate to commercial exploitation, although in recent years there have been attempts to enclose (temporarily) ground for private financial gain. The Society, backed by many residents, has resisted these. Although not always welcomed by everybody the funfairs and circuses have always been regarded as having, by custom and practice, been established before the Heath passed into modern legal controls. The London Marathon, established 1981, has joined that protected band of activities but it occupies only a small part of the Heath and that for a mere 36 hours once a year.

The Society also campaigns for improvements to the Heath, and it is pleasing to acknowledge a handful of major improvements over the years, for instance, the closure of several busy roads and their replacement by foot and cycle paths in 1999, and the adoption of a restricted grass cutting regime to create meadow areas first started in 1990, but being extended further this year. The appearance of the Heath has been further enhanced by the construction and seeding of bunds along the edges of several of the roads, initially along Charlton Way and sections of Shooters Hill Road (the A2) and then more recently along some of Prince Charles and Goffers Roads. These raised beds of wild flowers on the edges of the Heath fields help keep unwanted traffic away from the greensward and this year the displays have been remarkable. The weather in 2013 has also encouraged growth and we have the extra pleasure of the wild flower and grass meadows and the splendid ecological havens in Eliot Pits, Vanbrugh Pits and on the Hyde Vale slopes. Long may they flourish!

The Society was also proud in 2012 to promote and contribute to the installation of the "hub" on the Heath, much improving an untidy area and commemorating multiple events: the Royal Jubilee, the Olympic Games, and the 75th anniversary of the Society.

The Society is very grateful for the hard work of volunteers that goes into protecting the Heath. I must particularly thank Neil Rhind, Blackheath's historian for compiling this guide, working jointly with long-standing committee member **Dr Roger Marshall**. Neil was also largely responsible for the earlier Village trail booklet, mentioned above, and has published other well-known books on Blackheath. I would also like to thank Allan Griffin, Ruth Le Guen and Jo Swadkin for their invaluable help with this project, which is funded by a grant from the Heritage Lottery Fund.

Howard Shields
Chairman
November 2013

Blackheath ladies watching cricket, 1930. Francis Dodd

Background to the Heath

Blackheath is a 112 hectare (275 acre) open treeless plain, more or less in all these measures. It is one of London's best-known landmarks and, along with Greenwich Park, one of the most popular places of recreation and sporting activity in the capital - as it has been since the 13th century. During the last 300 years or so much of the rim of the Heath has been developed by buildings, many of considerable quality, which led Blackheath to be designated a conservation area in 1968 and, therefore, subject to protective legislation.

Before 1871 the Heath in all respects belonged to the Lords of the Manor, initially the Crown, but since the mid 17th century split unevenly between the Crown (north of the A2) and the Earls of Dartmouth (south of the A2), which prevails today. In 1871 both parties willingly gave the surface of the Heath into the protection of the then local authority: the Metropolitan Board of Works, which became in time the London County Council, then the Greater London Council. Currently, responsibility for its upkeep and management falls on the London Boroughs of Lewisham and Greenwich.

Earliest times

In the distant past the Heath was established as a scorched landscape after huge forest fires in the Weald of Kent destroyed much of the sylvan quality of what we call north-west Kent and south-east London.

As a result of these forest fires nothing much would grow for many centuries other than gorse. But as time went by sections of the Heath were taken for parkland and building purposes and the nature of the top soil enriched so that, in time, the suburb of Blackheath was developed, and shrubs, bushes and trees were encouraged to grow by land owners and gardeners.

Buildings and structures were erected around the Heath from the late 17th century onwards and by the 1870s the rim was complete; Greenwich Park wall having been built in 1619-1624 with, of course, parts replaced from time to time.

There were boundary disputes between the parishes of Greenwich and Lewisham, especially when the King's Surveyor, Samuel Travers, drew his plan of Blackheath showing the Manor of Greenwich boundary stretching far into Lewisham, thus claiming the area incorporating Dartmouth Row (*see below*) as part of Greenwich. The dispute was resolved in 1723, placing Dartmouth Row firmly in Lewisham, but surrendering a strip of land alongside St Germans Place and part of what was to become the Paragon ground to Greenwich. There are residents of the Dartmouth Row rectangle today who claim to be living in Greenwich, but largely because they enjoy an SE10 postal code.

Mapped roads and pathways wandered over Blackheath according to whichever plan you consult. The main Dover Road originally crept along the Greenwich Park Wall as Charlton Way, eventually joining the Old Dover Road and on to the Shooters Hill Road. By 1745, a desire line had been struck south from the south-west corner of Greenwich Park along the

4

Military display on the Heath, in 1943

line of the present A2 to join it at the north corner of St Germans Place: known from ancient times as Kidbrooke Corner.

Blackheath became a major location for the Crown and occupying forces to keep an eye on the Thames and travellers from the Kentish ports journeying to the capital – London. The highest part of Blackheath – The Point – is at least 38 metres (125ft) above mean sea level and affords magnificent views over London, the ever-changing prospect of the Capital still enjoyed today (2013).

The Heath enjoys well over a thousand years of recorded history which can be followed easily using the *Timeline* published with this walk (p 51). Blackheath is not common land - although the local population enjoys what are known as commoners' rights – it is manorial waste, largely owned by HM The Queen (roughly north of the A2) and the Earl of Dartmouth (most of the land south of the A2). Arguably, a few square metres of no great significance adjacent to Vanbrugh Park may have been owned by the estate of Sir Gregory Page in the 18th century.

There were disputes over boundaries between the manors and parishes of Greenwich and Lewisham from time to time. Our map shows the position of the boundary "crosses" put up in the 15th or 16th centuries.

Encroachments

The Heath's original size was probably about 304 hectares (750 acres) but encroachments, some illegal, over the centuries have reduced that considerably. The first major change in relatively modern times came in 1432 when Humphrey of Gloucester (1391-1447), brother of Henry V (1387-1422), fenced off 74 hectares (183 acres) of the Heath for what became, after his untimely death, Royal Greenwich Park. In the late 17th century the Legge family lawfully enclosed a sizeable section on the west side, which became the Dartmouth Row estate.

In the 1770s the Dartmouth estate enclosed a plot for a substantial house and private park, bounded by the roads now named The Orchard and Orchard Drive and Eliot Vale on the south. A chance to return this to the Heath in the 1890s was ignored. At about the same time two major plots were enclosed: the Holly Hedge House enclosure (now the TAVR camp) for a windmill and houses, and in 1774 the sand pit of Blackheath Vale was graced by two working windmills on its rim. This led to development within the pit in the early 19th century.

Finally, in 1801, John Julius Angerstein (1735-1823) enclosed roughly 11 hectares (26 ½ acres) of what he claimed was waste land without a known owner. In fact the owner was the Crown and the Parish, but he squared the authorities with an annual fee of £10 (still being paid). Eventually, this plot was developed as that estate roughly within the west end of Shooters Hill Road, Vanbrugh Park, St John's Park and Stratheden Road.

There were other minor encroachments (all permanent) and these are touched on in the various walks described below.

Ecology (contributed by David Notton)

The natural history of the Heath has been determined by fast-draining soils which do not favour tree growth, resulting in fine open views. The most important, and often overlooked, habitat is acid grassland, with small but exquisite wild flowers in many areas. The reddish leaves of sheep's sorrel, food of the small copper butterfly, are typical and harebells and waxcap fungi can be seen. Bare and disturbed ground is important for rare annuals such as clustered clover, and provides basking and nesting sites for solitary bees. The slopes of Hyde Vale and the disused sand pits have unusual lichen communities surviving in short unshaded grassland, and a rich insect fauna especially among the gorse of Vanbrugh Pits and the spring fed grassland of Eliot Pits.

The seasonal pond at Whitefield's Mount (see below) is notable, supporting trifid bur-marigold, as well as frogs, toads and newts. Invasive trees are a threat, such as the non-native Holm oak which shades out wildflowers, as well as rubbish dumping, and pollution from increasingly busy roads. However, recent changes such as late grass cutting to allow wild flowers to seed will enhance the particular beauty of the Heath.

Fauna

Inevitably, a wide open space will attract large numbers of birds and the Heath is no exception. Flocks have rested on Blackheath in varying numbers over the decades. Gulls, crows, starlings, pigeons and blackbirds have all found a home here. The wild areas at Eliot and Vanbrugh Pits and Hyde Vale are home to a great variety of birds, some quite rare for the locality like chiff-chaff, spotted flycatcher and blackcap. The Prince of Wales pond, with its relatively new duck island, is home to mallards, swans, moorhens and ever increasing numbers of Canada geese (the latter not always welcome). Herons make regular calls to the Prince of Wales and Hare & Billet ponds from their nests in neighbouring parks and ponds. The rare Egyptian goose is an occasional visitor.

Of the mammals the urban fox is the dominant specie; hedgehogs disappeared 30 or more years ago. Urban badger and muntjack deer have not been spotted – yet. *Lucanus servus* (the stag beetle, indigenous to Blackheath and the largest of its type in Britain) is familiar among insect life but over-manicured urban gardens have caused a serious decline.

The management of the Heath

When the Greater London Council was abolished in 1986, the responsibility for running the Heath was split between the two boroughs of Lewisham and Greenwich with the major share south of the A2 going to Lewisham. Within two years, it was appreciated that there was much to be gained from a common approach particularly for the coordination of any events, such as fairs and circuses, and this led to the formation of the Blackheath Joint Working Party.

Membership presently consists of three local councillors from each borough, one of whom is elected as the chairman, as well as representatives from the three major local amenity societies and other interested groups. Officers from the two boroughs and from Glendale, who maintain the Heath for Lewisham, also attend. The Working Party meets at least five times a year and one of these meetings is for the general public.

At these meetings, it offers advice to the boroughs on such matters as the maintenance and improvement of the grassland, the meadows and the ponds on the Heath, as well as on any activities taking place or events. In 2011, both councils adopted a special Blackheath Events Policy which defined the criteria for the consideration of events proposed on the Heath and the role of the Working Party in their assessment.

Apostrophes in street names

The authors have followed the convention whereby street names in use before, roughly, the mid 19th century (e.g. Grotes Place) do not take the apostrophe, and those of the 20th century do.

Introduction to the Walks

This guide gives you three walks around Blackheath, each of which can be undertaken separately or in combination with any one of the others. Two of these walks start from Blackheath Village on the southern side of the Heath, whilst the third starts from the opposite side at the gates to Greenwich Park near to Shooters Hill Road (A2).

The map on the page opposite the beginning of each walk indicates the subsequent route.

1. The West Walk:
The starting point for this is the north end of Tranquil Vale in Blackheath Village and it passes the Hare and Billet pub and Holly Hedge House before crossing over Shooters Hill Road (A2). It then visits the Point and the prominent Rangers House before ending at Blackheath Gate, which is the main southern entrance to Greenwich Park. This should take about an hour with normal walking, although if you are stopping to identify and study any of the buildings or features it will clearly take much longer.

2. The East Walk:
This starts where the first walk ends, namely at the Blackheath Gate and takes you past the Gibb Memorial to Vanbrugh Terrace and St Germans Place, before returning to Blackheath Village via the famous Georgian Paragon and the Princess of Wales pub. This walk will take about 45 minutes.

3. The Central Walk:
This starts in Royal Parade at All Saints' Church on the Heath and goes in a northerly direction along Duke Humphrey Road, over the new central Hub of the Heath to the Blackheath Gate to the Park. This is a very short walk (15 minutes), even including its diversion into Blackheath Vale, so it can be combined with either of the other two if desired.

If you know Blackheath already you will have no trouble in following the roads as indicated on the maps and shown in sequence in the summaries at the end of each walk. However, it would be more attractive in many ways to walk freely on the Heath itself and away from most of the traffic. The major buildings and other visible features can then be identified as you go by their numbers on the maps, their photographs or, again, from the appropriate summaries. All are also highlighted in bold in the main text.

The history of the Heath is divided into 18 short sections, numbered as you proceed clockwise around the Heath and matching the route and order of the walks. If you are new to the area, you may prefer to follow the detailed walking instructions, which are in italics at the head of each section, and which will lead you around each of the shorter walks. In this case it is suggested that you identify the buildings and features from the bold type in the text or from the map as you go, and at the end of a walk retire to the comfort of an armchair to read the full historic context of what you have just seen.

However, an alternative approach to the full walks as above might be to settle on any one or two of the History Sections identified from the summaries or main text and read the full details, whilst you are in that location.

The Heath unmown in 2013

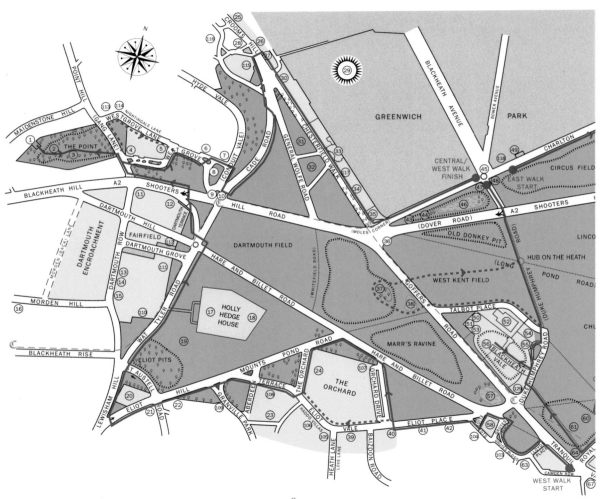

1. The West Walk

History Section 1: Tranquil Vale to the Hare and Billet Pub

Start of walk at the top of Tranquil Vale

The West Walk starts at the top, northern, end of Blackheath Village, where you can walk up Tranquil Vale towards the open Heath. Turn left when the road levels off into Lloyds Place and follow the building line around the rectangle of grass, along Grotes Buildings and then around the corner to the north to the Hare and Billet public house.

The south boundary of the Heath was once marked by the stream called the Upper Kid Brook, running east to west off Shooters Hill, through the Village and on to Lewisham, where it joins the River Quaggy. This natural water course is now in a concrete pipe and the parish boundary is marked by the railway metals of the North Kent line. Long before the railway arrived some of the ground between Lloyds Place and Eliot Vale was in agricultural use, but from the early 18th century there was a creeping process of infill by a cluster of small houses and the public house (which survives) called the Hare & Billet (*see below*).

Land ownership was complicated: Lloyds Place, Grotes Place and the horseshoe-shaped green between them were part of the Dartmouth Estate; Grotes Buildings stood in the Manor of Old Court, purchased by John Morden in 1699 from the Crown. Eliot Place and Eliot Vale were part of the land belonging to the Eliot family, later the Earls of St Germans.

There was a small group of houses at the top of Tranquil Vale and around the corner into Lloyds Place by the 1750s, perhaps before. It was Dartmouth territory, but must have once been part of the waste of the Heath. The dominant building is **Eastnor House**, a structure here by 1750 but much enlarged and fashioned over the decades after 1780, the

Eastnor House in Lloyds Place

drum-shaped front entrance possibly created later in the 18th century. Lloyds Place takes its name from John Lloyd once a resident of No 3.

Morden College trustees came into the land on the south-west side of the green - known as Ancock's Hill Field or Hilly Field for no reason discovered to date - through its ownership of the Queen's Lands – purchased by John Morden to provide an endowment for his College (new built on the south-east edge of the Heath in 1695- *see below*). The College trustees granted a lease to Andrew Grote (1710-1788), of Point House (*see below*) to develop the ground and this was undertaken in 1773. Alas, the houses were on College land, but the front gardens were on the Heath - Dartmouth territory; so a deal had to be made between the parties, not resolved until the 1820s.

No 3 Grotes Buildings was the home of the golfer William Innes (1719-1795), whose portrait is one of the most famous in sporting art, although the original was lost in a fire at the Siege of Lucknow (1857). **No 6** was the base in 1937 for the social research foundation known as Mass Observation. The west end of Grotes Buildings boasted a stable and coach house block for all the tenants and, later, commercial premises for blacksmiths and farriers. This was demolished in 1892 for a horse bus stable for transport magnate Thomas Tilling (1825-1893). Eventually extended and converted into an electrical factory in 1921, it was demolished in December 1995 and the present **Nos 19-26 Eliot Place** erected on the site by 2001-2002.

The tongue of land sticking out towards the Heath was developed by 1733 – Stubbs Buildings – but by 1765 the foremost building was the public house by then known as the **Hare & Billet**. Some claim it is a corruption of the sign Harrow & Billet, but there is no prima facie evidence for this. Behind the pub was a row of cottages called the *Blue Houses*, probably made of mud and finished in blue tinted limewash. These went down to be replaced by Grotes Place and Eliot Cottages, built on the other side,

Hare & Billet pub. in 1904

facing west. The distinctive corner house (**No 1 Grotes Place**) with the bow window dates from 1810. Next door is the remains of the building **(No 2)** known as the **Canister House -** of uncertain date but certainly before 1780.

Immediately opposite the pub is the **Hare & Billet pond**. Although in the south-east corner of Marr's Ravine, an abandoned gravel pit, it is included here because the pond was a watering place for cattle and horses, the drovers taking their refreshment at the neighbouring inn. The location of the pond is marked more or less on Samuel Travers' 1695 plan of Blackheath with the legend "Beggar's Bush", so the pond and the pub may have been attracting customers from the 17th century, if not before. For many years, there was a retaining rail to prevent too many animals wading into the pond and fouling the water. Because of the water a small grove of trees and shrubs has flourished, particularly crack willows. The pond has not been known to completely dry out even in very hot weather so it may be fed by a land spring. Recently, several large fish have been introduced and seem to be thriving. Notices discouraging fishing have been erected.

On the Heath to the north, **Marr's Ravine** was an important location for the Blackheath golfers – the second hole was close to the north end of Orchard Drive, and the tee off for the third hole was a few yards west of the Hare & Billet Pond, with the hole being close to the Old Donkey Pit (*see below*). When the Golf Club moved its match play to Eltham in 1923, Marr's Ravine lost its sporting interest but was, occasionally, one of the

Golfers hitting across Marr's Ravine

Heath's temporary ponds and much appreciated by small boys. Much of the west end of the Ravine was infilled with spoil in 1905 during the installation of the Great Sewer, which runs from west to east underneath the Heath.

Wartime needs led to the remains of the Ravine being filled in completely and consolidated. Until the late 1990s Marr's Ravine was separated from Dartmouth Field to its west by a section of Mounts Pond Road, but the misuse of the road as a car park, and the erosion caused by vehicles driving over the Heath, encouraged it to be dug up and turfed over in 2000 retaining only a footpath width.

History Section 2: Hare & Billet Pub to Mounts Pond Road

It is probably too early in the walk to tarry at the pub so choose between following the buildings around two sides of a triangle (Eliot Place, Orchard Drive) or cut across using the hypotenuse, which is Hare and Billet Road, and then turn left into Mounts Pond Road.

If you choose the former route you may prefer, when you come to the end of Eliot Place, to take the short cut down and up through Eliot Vale. This way you will see two fine houses, the entrance to the intriguing Heath Lane, a view of the Pagoda from the top of Pagoda Gardens and you will then rejoin the latter route at the eastern end of Aberdeen Terrace.

The terrace behind the public house – Eliot Cottages – was built by Lewis Glenton (1812-1873) in 1857. At the east end of Eliot Place there is a pair of cottages orné (**Nos 14-15 Eliot Place**), built as an investment by HRH Princess Caroline's major domo, John Jacob Sicard, by 1802 (*See also Montague House, below*). Sicard lived in one for a brief period. The triangle of grass to the front of the site was once considered a suitable place for the new Blackheath church – **All Saints'**. Unfortunately for the church authorities, the local residents petitioned the Earl of Dartmouth to suggest another site. This was done and the church, designed by Benjamin Ferrey (1810-1880) was erected on the present plot, closer to the Village, off Royal Parade, in 1857-58 and well away from a public house and the carters' watering hole for both themselves and the horses. The principal southern stretch of the Heath frame is from Eliot Place to Eliot Hill. Until the late 1780s the ground, stretching down to the Kid Brook, was in farm use, but in 1792 the Eliot trustees granted a

Eliot Place in 1852

Eliot Place in 2011

development lease to Alexander Doull. Doull (1753-1821) was probably responsible for the three-storey blocks of semi-detached houses in the Place but not for **No 1 (Heathfield House)** nor **No 6 Eliot Place**.

Heathfield House may have been the design work of Michael Searles (1751-1813), creator of The Paragon and South Row, but there is no evidence for this, other than circumstantial, discovered to date. **No 6** was the home and observatory of astronomer Stephen Groombridge (1755-1832) from 1812 to his death. Polar explorer Sir James Clark Ross (1800-1862) lived at **No 2** in the 1840s, and a Blue Plaque marks his residence there.

The Heath opposite provided a very convenient pleasure ground and when, inevitably, most of the houses of Eliot Place at some time or other went into school use, the Heath became the playground and sports' field for, mostly, boys. The girls did not play games. The best known school was that of Dr John Potticary (1763-1820) at Nos 1 & 2 early in the 19th century (Benjamin Disraeli was a pupil here briefly) and it was moved by his nephew, the Rev George Potticary (1796-1863) to **No 9 Eliot Place,** where it flourished in educational use until 1908, held by a succession of proprietors. By 1910, No 9 was worn out by generations of boys and it was demolished for Nos 9a and 9b. Its swimming pool and additional school room was later added to the title of No 10.

The games known to have been played on the Heath here were hockey, various forms of football (with a variety of rules or none), shinty, cricket and possibly a little schoolboy golf. The Blackheath Golf Club's greens did not stretch so far south. In any event, Marr's Ravine was once sufficiently enlarged to present a serious hazard – sometimes filling with water during very wet weather, much to the enjoyment of small boys.

The north side of Eliot Vale, the houses of which date from about 1894, was the south boundary of the Orchard House estate. Orchard House was another Dartmouth family property, no doubt once part of the Heath. Dartmouth estate managers first fenced it for an orchard and then, in 1784, authorised the building of a substantial house by West Indies merchant

Duncan Campbell (1741-1803). Campbell was an enthusiastic golfer (one-time Captain of the Blackheath Society of Goffers) but was also Commissioner of Convicts at Woolwich. He chose the convicts needed for the transportations to Australia which started in May 1787.

Once Campbell had left, the Dartmouth trustees refashioned the house adding a long stable block in 1801. Orchard House was occupied largely by members of the Dartmouth family until the mid 1850s. Having passed through various aristocratic hands, it was part of the estate of the 5th Earl of Dartmouth when he died in 1891. This led to a vigorous public campaign to remove the house and restore the ground to the Heath. Alas, the Dartmouth agents were not moved and abandoned Orchard House to developers D & R Kennard in 1893 who laid out the houses of Eliot Vale, The Orchard and Orchard Drive. The big house remained but was converted into flats in 1920/21 – eventually to be demolished in 1965

The Pagoda in 2013

for the block of flats called **Lynn Court**. A little bit of infill on the north side in the late 1930s did nothing for the aesthetics of the Orchard estate. But the biggest damage came in 1963-64 when No 1 The Orchard was demolished for a three storey concrete and glass block called **North Several**, designed by architect Royston Summers (1931-2012) for a group of enthusiasts who had originally lived in the Span Development in South Row.

Until the Orchard estate was developed in the 1890s, Eliot Vale was part of the south boundary to the Heath so, having walked around the Orchard rectangle, the reader can dally at the entrance to **Heath Lane** (erstwhile Love Lane until 1939). Here they will see the much-altered sections of **The Close** (originally known as West Lodge), designed by architect William James Green (1856-1899) for his brother ship owner Joseph Fletcher Green (1847-1921). It was a wedding present from his mother-in-law (Mrs Ellen Penn), on the marriage of her daughter, also Ellen, to Joseph in 1880.

Next to the Close to the east is **No 8 Eliot Vale** (Eliot Vale House) of 1805 (not 1780 as the plaque on the building) and Eliot Vale Cottage (**No 9 Eliot Vale**). They were built by developer Alexander Doull (1760-1817) (*see also Eliot Place, above*)], on a lease from the Eliot trustees (the Earls of St Germans) on a stretch of land called the Slipe. It was not the best building plot because it was wet more often than not with water draining off the Heath to the Upper Kid Brook in the Valley below. Some of this ground had been part of the Heath so it was necessary for Doull to pay a small annual fine for his encroachment. Long before the houses were built, the thickets here were the haunt of gipsies and travellers.

History Section 3: Aberdeen Terrace to Eliot Hill

Again you can follow the line of the buildings (The Orchard, Aberdeen Terrace) or cut across into Eliot Hill using Mounts Pond Road.

The next point of Heath interest is Aberdeen Terrace, a grand statement of 10 substantial semi-detached villas, built for developer Lewis Glenton

to the design of architect John Whichcord Jnr (1823-1885). From the 1930s, **Nos 7** and **8 Aberdeen Terrace** were taken into use as offices by

Aberdeen Terrace in 2013

the National Union of Public Employees (NUPE). After the union staff left, the two buildings were restored as somewhat grand single family houses by architect Philip Cooper.

The Aberdeen Terrace development was on the gardens and stables of the Chinese style pavilion, **The Pagoda**, the curved roof of which can still just be seen from the Heath but is better studied from its entrance in Pagoda Gardens. This was designed as a garden pavilion for Henry Scott, 3rd Duke of Buccleuch and his wife Elizabeth (1744-1827) daughter of the Earl of Cardigan, by architect Sir William Chambers (1723-1796) in 1762-1763.

Lewis Glenton obtained a lease in 1853 and extended the house for his own purposes, and used the extensive gardens on the north side for Aberdeen Terrace and what were originally known from 1857-58 as Haddo Villas, but now more prosaically as **Nos 1-6 Eliot Vale**. The naming of these groups of buildings was because Glenton was a bit of snob and his across-the-Heath neighbour, in Rangers House, was – from time to time - George Gordon Hamilton, Lord Haddo and 4th Earl of Aberdeen (1816-1864), one-time Prime Minister.

Going back now to the Heath and walking down Mounts Pond Road you will see to your left at the top of Granville Park, a fine middle class development of villas largely intact. Three of the best face the Heath and, unusually, boast no street numbers; from left to right: **Granville House, Newton House** and **Clarendon House**. The triangles of grass on the north sides have developed a considerable thicket of trees and shrubs.

Further down the road on the next corner is the fine and extraordinary house once known as The Knoll. After a wing was cut off for an independent house, the smaller section was called **The Knoll**, and the larger **The Old Knoll**. The core of the house dates from 1798 when it was designed by architect George Gibson (c1740-1810) on the Nole Field. The east wing was added for a billiard room in about 1855. Despite its gloomy appearance on the north elevation, where the windows look straight into a bank of the Heath, a finer prospect can be seen from the south elevation in Oakcroft Road. In 1854 the large pleasure garden and meadow were chopped off the title and developed for Granville Park, infilling the natural coombe or valley. The smaller retained garden was further truncated with the building in 1903 of Oakcroft Road, when the original Knoll house was cut into two unequal sections. A cast-iron London County Council boundary marker can still be seen against the Old Knoll garden wall.

On your right fronting Eliot Hill are the **Eliot Pits**, abandoned gravel workings from the late 17th / early 18th century. The scarp of the pit was retained and protected by a rail (since removed) when the Heath was taken into care in 1871 and the whole ground allowed to grow wild, a little like Vanbrugh Pits and Hyde Vale on the north side of the Heath, but more dramatic. Attempts by local authorities to utilise this natural theatre-shaped ecologically rich hollow for a swimming pool were frustrated in 1922; other schemes over the years were also seen off, on the grounds that Eliot Pits is a remarkable survival in urban London and, anyway, children like playing in the thickets as they are. The most recent in 2013 was for a children's play space and resulted in the commissioning of an ecological study with the consultant's report not recommending its use.

Eliot Pits off Eliot Hill

South of the Pits, across Eliot Hill and St Austell Road (the Cornish connection to the landowner here – the Eliots, of St Germans) is a remarkable feature: **The Hermitage**, a block of flats actually placed on the Heath. A grant from the Dartmouth Estate to Joseph Still in 1756 led to a large wooden house on the plot, which was replaced twice, firstly in 1872. The last version being demolished in 1936 for the present Hermitage flats, designed by architect Eric Ebel, of Wembley Park. At the rear of the Hermitage, near St Austell Road, is a land spring which keeps this section of grass lush and the trees flourishing with a good risk of getting ones feet wet.

Opposite the Hermitage from 1807 until 1910 was a mansion called **Eliot Lodge,** designed by architect Robert Smirke (1781-1867) for General Sir Alexander Hope (1769-1837) when the latter was Commandant at the Royal Artillery at Woolwich. It lost some of its garden for the lower houses on Eliot Hill (Nos 1-6) and Eliot Park in 1865. The house footprint was replaced by the Edwardian style villas **(Nos 7 to 12)** in 1911. Alas, no useful pictures of Eliot Lodge have been discovered.

You can now turn right or north if you prefer, either into St. Austell Road or Lewisham Hill. Either will lead you into Wat Tyler Road and you should follow this north, passing Holly Hedge House on your right and Grey Ladies Gardens, Dartmouth Court and Dartmouth Terrace on your left, until you come to Shooters Hill Road. This you can then cross at the nearby pedestrian traffic lights.

Wat Tyler Road is named (in the 1930s) after the leader of the failed Peasants' Revolt, who met representatives of King Richard II on Blackheath in 1381 (see Heath *Timeline*). The first construction you will see on your left in this road is the brick wall of a modern development called **Greyladies Gardens**. It was built in the late 1960s on the garden of Dartmouth House, in Dartmouth Row. The College of Greyladies was an Anglican social welfare group founded in the 1880s.

To the right (eastwards) is the large 1 hectare (2 ½ acre) enclosure of **Holly Hedge House**. It was never part of the Heath as we know it today, because it was enclosed very early in the ownership of the Legge (Dartmouth) family for a windmill and a miller's house. The earliest date we know is 1723 but, in due course, the mill and the miller left and the house was replaced (or restructured) in 1770 by a substantial property called Holly Hedge House. This name, no doubt, because its boundary was marked by railings and a holly hedge. From 1804 to 1887 this was to become a home for the Vicars of Lewisham: there was Henry Legge (1767-1827), son of the 2nd Earl of Dartmouth (1731-1801); and he was followed here in 1843 by another Henry Legge (1804-1887), this time the 5th son of the 3rd Earl of Dartmouth (1755-1810).

When Henry died in February 1887, the house fell empty and was of not much interest to the Dartmouth trustees - they owned enough empty properties as it was. However, all this coincided with the local Volunteer Militia (rifles and artillerymen) seeking a substantial new headquarters. They took Holly Hedge House and have remained there in some form or other ever since. The initial deal was set in 1888 for a 30 year lease. In 1906 the Volunteers made a good offer and the freehold passed to the corps and it has remained with their successors (presently the TAVR). It provides a drill shed, an officers' mess and plenty of space for exercises and an encampment.

During the Great War of 1914-1918 Holly Hedge was a major local recruitment centre; in 1939-1945 it was the centre base for the London Defences encompassing Ack-ack guns, searchlights, barrage balloons

Rear of Holly Hedge House in 1938

and the Z-rocket batteries. So many men were engaged that extra accommodation in the form of Nissen Huts had to be built on the Heath. Within the compound are the remains of the old Holly Hedge House, part damaged during the war and the residue largely pulled down by the Army. There is a memorial to volunteers and territorials, who fell in the world wars, and a Coade stone lion (recently removed to the Greenwich Tourism Centre), which is a replica of part of the Nelson victory frieze on the old Royal Naval College, now in part the University of Greenwich. The more modern block to the south was built by the War Office as married quarters for full-time regulars stationed at Woolwich.

This section was sold to the private sector in recent years and is now called Tyler House. Holly Hedge House was used as a Metropolitan Police command HQ during the XXXth Modern Olympiad in 2012 and a battery of Rapier surface-to-air missiles was also stationed just outside on the Heath.

Rapier missiles defending Dartmouth Terrace

A short distance further along on your left is **Dartmouth Court**, which replaced the 1750s Red House in 1935-36 and was designed by architects Annesley, Brownrigg & Hiscock. One of the outstanding historic landmarks on Blackheath is the white stone-faced **Lydia and Sherwell houses** between Dartmouth Grove and Dartmouth Hill. The structures

Dartmouth Court (on the left) and Lydia and Sherwell Houses

date from 1776 and are one of the earliest pairs of semi-detached houses known. They boast fine interiors and cantilevered stone staircases.

Since 1854 the north-west prospect has been stopped by the five grand houses now called **Dartmouth Terrace**, built by developer Lewis Glenton, on the remains of a bowling green and once part of the **Green Man Hotel** and public house. The north side facing across to West Grove was covered with another Glenton scheme called Lansdowne Place, but this was demolished in 1969-1970.

Hare and Billet Pond with Dartmouth Terrace behind

On your right on the Heath is **Dartmouth Field,** which has been laid down for cricket games from the early 19th century until almost the present day. In the late 17th century a watch tower had been erected here, about 100 yards east from Dartmouth Terrace. Whether this was part of the infrastructure for the twice yearly cattle fairs held since 1683 in the vicinity and around the Holly Hedge House windmill enclosure, is not known. It may have been an observation post allied to the experiments with the mortars and bombs at Whitefield's Mount in 1687. Dartmouth Field was split by a footpath which expanded by stealth into a metalled highway – Whitefield Road – but this was closed, along with Long Pond Road and other Heath rat runs, around 2000 and returned to its natural state.

Green Man Hotel (1688-1868) on Blackheath Hill

The visual appearance of this field and several other sections of the Heath have also been much enriched by a restricted grass cutting regime. This was successfully started on the Vanbrugh Pits by Greenwich Council and then adopted by Lewisham most obviously at Paragon Field off St Germans Place in 1990. It involves cutting only once or, occasionally, twice a year. Then collecting the mown grass thus, in the long run impoverishing the acid grassland leading to the growth of many fine grass species and indigenous wild flowers. These summer meadows were extended in 2013 to include parts of Dartmouth Field adjacent to the A2 with corridors down to Whitefield's Mount and the Hare & Billet pond, as well as most of Riding Field in the east.

History Section 5: The Point

Cross over Shooters Hill Road (A2) at the pedestrian lights at the end of Dartmouth Terrace, turn left and walk parallel to the main road until you come to the top of Blackheath Hill. Turn right here and continue until you come to the junction of Point Hill and West Grove. The green open space on your left is The Point.

This "forgotten" part of Blackheath and part of the Royal Manor was known in the past as Maidenstone Hill. In the early 18th century it was

Whilst you are in Dartmouth Field or on the equivalent open grassland to the north of Shooters Hill Road note the relative inconsequence of the almost continuous traffic; this is due to shielding of the noise by the bunds or raised earth mounds, which run parallel to the road. These were installed by Transport for London in the spring of 2009 as part of a major reconstruction of the road; they followed designs for the management of the Heath by Kim Wilkie Associates published in a report commissioned principally by English Heritage in 2003.

The bunds deflect sound upward and wild flowers sown on their tops help block the view of the moving traffic. Pedestrians and cyclists also benefited with the establishment of a new shared pathway to the north of the road. Parking, particularly of heavy goods vehicles taking a break on route to Dover which was indiscriminate here, has also been eliminated by discreet rows of wooden posts. This design has been copied elsewhere on less important roads across the Heath with notable success, and it is hoped that this great improvement for Heath users will be extended further in the years to come.

The caverns in the mid 19th century

judged by the trustees of Morden College as part of the Queen's Lands – which were bought by John Morden from the Crown in 1699. (*See also Grote's Buildings, above*). Beneath the Point were deposits of chalk and these were exploited, supposedly as early as the 10th century but mostly not until the 17th and 18th century, creating large underground **caverns**. Much nonsense has been generated about these caves including that Greenwich residents hid in them when the Danes invaded – they were allegedly known as Dene- or Dane-holes. Jack Cade and Dick Turpin supposedly hid in the caverns from time to time. The entrance was in Maidenstone Hill and the cavity was much exploited for entertainment in the early 19th century. But for safety reasons after a near disaster when the lights were doused, they were closed and the entrance consolidated. It was last opened formally in 1939 to consider the caverns' use as air raid shelters – they were found wanting, unlike the caves at Chislehurst.

During the mid 18th century the trustees of Morden College authorised the building of houses on the edges of the highway waste facing Blackheath Hill and, eventually, Maidenstone Hill. In 1751 the Crown took legal action (which went on for years) and finally stopped the exploitation but allowed the existing houses to remain. The central plain was to remain open and the Point, as part of the Crown waste of Blackheath, was encompassed by the legislation of 1869 and 1871, which took Blackheath into public care in perpetuity for the people of London. It offers one of the best prospects of London from its now slightly off-centre **Viewpoint**. The trees and thickets surrounding the Point are relatively modern from the overgrowth of neighbouring gardens on Blackheath Hill and Maidenstone Hill, to which there are footpaths. In recent Months (2017) the area has been much improved and a new sign (by Peter Kent) erected.

When you have finished admiring the views, read the inscription on the nearby boulder dedicated on 28 June 2013 to an RAF Hurricane pilot, Flight Lieutenant Richard Reynell, who was killed near this spot on 7 September 1940. This is a poignant **memorial** partly because of his age (28) and partly because he came all the way from Australia to fight the enemies of Britain and the free European nations.

Battle of Britain Memorial

History Section 6: Point Hill to Hyde Vale

*Retrace your footsteps across **The Point** to **Point Hill** and then stay on the Heath and take in **West Grove** which is numbered from east to west. Walk east along **West Grove** until you come to **Hyde Vale**. An interesting alternative route away from the present Heath frontage is to go a few yards down **Point Hill** and then turn right into **West Grove Lane**. After a short distance you will rejoin the main route.*

The roadway here was originally known, in 1700, as The Grove and then it became Chocolate Row, then the Grove again, but reverted to West Grove in 1938. This section and the top (south-west) end of Hyde Vale were once owned by the Mason family, of Crooms Hill. The land was sold to Sir Ambrose Crowley in 1717 – and through family arrangements transferred because Elizabeth Crowley had married John, Earl of Ashburnham. He took over control of her property as of right. There were Heath encroachments here by 1699 and at least 20 quality dwellings by the early 18th century. None survives.

No 18 (Point House): This house built for John Hoare, the banker, probably dates from 1734, but was altered later in the 18th century. A large number of rich and distinguished families, including Andrew Grote (1710-1788), a German banker, whose name is remembered across the Heath in Grotes Buildings and Grotes Place, lived here. In the early 19th century it was

Point House Hotel in 1939

fitted out as a private observatory by John Walker (1732-1806), with an Equatorial Room and Mathematical Pillar. Note the observation window on the third floor. Point House was the West Kent & Greenwich Carlton Club from 1880 to 1926 and a hotel thereafter until 1940. The very fine listed iron railings were stolen in the 1939-1945 war. The House is now in flats.

Nos. 14-18 West Grove were developments by the trustees of Morden College on a wheat field once owned by farmer John Hatch as early as the 1690s. **No 14** was called The Crosslets and then Hamilton House, and dates from about 1740, when it was built for Deptford shipbuilder Peter Bronsden (d1745). It was the home of retired whaling ship-owner Samuel Enderby (1718-1797) until his death; then of Twinings, the tea merchants, and the Knill family from 1850 and for the next 70 years, who called the house: The Crosslets.

Nos 15 & 16 of 1885 are on the site of Cambridge House, a fine red brick mansion of 1739, which was destroyed by fire in 1881. The staircase was decorated by John, son of the notable artist James Thornhill (1675-1734), who painted the Dining Hall, in Greenwich Hospital. **No 17** was designed by architect Michael Searles (1751-1813) in 1790 on the site of

West Grove: from No 14 (left) to No 6 (right)

an earlier house. In the 20th century, from 1900 to 1960 it was famous as a nursing home called Manna Mead.

Nos 9-12 of 1875 were designed by Greenwich architect Herbert Williams (1810-1873). **Nos 11-12** were bought by Goldsmiths' College in 1912 for student hostel use, eventually adding Nos 9 and 10 as extra dormitory accommodation.

No 6 was restored by the Blackheath Preservation Trust in 1939 because of the loss of **No 5 (Bexley House)** for the undistinguished replacement immediately to the west. **Nos 6-7-8** are of the mid 18th century. No 7 was extended forward with a Victorian porch.

Nos 3 & 4 are on the site of the **Chocolate House**, a place of fashionable assembly and entertainment opened by Thomas and Grace Tozier in 1702, who claimed to be chocolate makers to the King. It was hugely successful and remained with their descendants until purchased by restaurateur Charles Walker in 1776. In 1788, he moved his enterprise across the road to the **Green Man Public House and Assembly Rooms** taking the best clients with him. The Chocolate House eventually became a boys' school in the 1790s, and it has since been claimed that it was the inspiration for Creakle's Academy, in *David Copperfield*, by Charles Dickens (1812-1870). Eventually, the front garden was sold for development (erstwhile Nos 3 & 4, later bombed). Thereafter it was Ashburnham House School, latterly for girls until its closure in 1877. The Chocolate House was demolished in 1887.

No 2 West Grove by Thomas Leverton (1743-1824) is roughly of 1780 and since altered.

No 1 (Conduit House) was originally a colonnaded house of about 1804, but was demolished in 1936 and replaced by the present corner block.

Conduit Head in 2013

It takes its name from the ancient **conduit head** erected about 1710 on the corner of West Grove and Hyde Vale. The head was an entrance to a series of brick tunnels which led from Blackheath down to Greenwich to channel clean water draining off the Heath to the Royal Seamen's Hospital (now Greenwich University) by the Thames. The largest conduit head in the district can be found in a substantial building - the Standard Reservoir - on the west side of Greenwich Park, opposite the top of Crooms Hill where railings have taken over from the wall.

A diversion: West Grove Lane, until 1938 called Nightingale Lane (named after a man, not the songbird), was part of the original north boundary of the Heath, forming the footway from Point Hill (Gang Lane) to the Greenwich Park Wall. With the development by Morden College of Nos 14 to 18 West Grove, it became a service mews for those houses. Other than **No 1** (**West Grove House**), of about 1780, nothing was to follow until **West Grove Terrace** was built on the east garden of the House in 1876. Further to the east a couple of modest houses and some modern infill were built to take advantage of the views of Greenwich and beyond, and have little connection to the Heath as such.

West Grove House & Terrace

At Conduit House cross over Hyde Vale and walk a few yards towards Shooters Hill Road to observe the drinking fountain and then east along Cade Road until you come to Crooms Hill, where you will see signs for Chesterfield Gardens and the Manor House on the left hand side.

On the Heath, where Hyde Vale joins West Grove and opposite **Conduit House** (1937), was a sizeable pond, once the largest on the Heath and known as Real or Royal Pond and eventually Chocolate Pond (*see West Grove, above*). It was a problem because the ground was much churned up by the thousands of cattle driven to its edge for refreshment. Greenwich Parish was constantly nagged about its dirty state: mud, malodorous rubbish, dead animals, a favourite place for suicides and even for the victims of robbery and murder. For 40 years the complaints continued, although in 1864 the local Board of Works claimed it was full and clean. The newly-placed **horse trough**, supplied by the Metropolitan Horse & Cattle Trough Society and the **drinking fountain** at the edge of the

Cattle trough in memoriam Robert Trotter Esq, 1877

Shooters Hill Road, saw a diminution in the use of the Chocolate Pond, which was then dredged, filled in and consolidated by the Metropolitan Board of Works in 1878. The abundance of trees on the Heath at this point may tell us something.

This southern end of Hyde Vale was known as Conduit Vale until 1881, when the summit was eased and the road widened. It has suffered a considerable amount of development and rebuilding since the mid 1740s to the present day. Hyde Vale proper (named after the family of John Hyde, landowners hereabouts in the mid 18th-century) was simply the north end of the road at the outset.

Walking along Cade Road you will now see another of the overgrown sections of the Heath, but it is not as ancient as the Vanbrugh Pits or Eliot Pits. The natural combe which is Hyde Vale enjoyed steep sides on its east side and, over the years, 1900 to the 1950s, this gradually grew wild and a substantial thicket has taken over the slopes. There are footpaths through the trees which lead down to Hyde Vale or along to the Girls' School (see below). Good prospects of London (including of St Paul's Cathedral) can be obtained from the top of the slopes. Cade Road itself commemorates the gathering on Blackheath of a rebellious peasant army led by Jack Cade in early June 1450 on their way into the City of London (see Heath **Timeline** below).

At the end of Cade Road there are several important buildings built on the waste of Blackheath. These include the magnificent **Manor House** which dates from the early 1690s (as do some of the houses on Crooms Hill to the north). This splendid Dutch-style Manor House survives. Alas, three others do not: they were Crooms Hill House, the Yews and Clifton House – all gone by 1938. They were replaced by the Beaver Housing Society development on **Wellington Gardens** and **Chesterfield Gardens**; part pre-war and part post-war. They were designed by architect William Braxton Sinclair (1883-1963), who successfully picked up the style of Crooms Hill House of 1720. The stone entrance arch to the original house was incorporated into the Crooms Hill frontage of

Only the Manor House on the right remains today

Chesterfield Gardens. Behind all these is the **St Ursula's School for Girls**, in a re-fashioned early 18th century building known variously as Wellington Grove, Hyde Cliff, or Rock House from the time it was owned by a family of publishers of that name. The Roman Catholic Order, which opened the school, took the building in 1893 and subsequently bought some adjacent Heath land on Crooms Hill from the Crown.

History Section 8: Crooms Hill to Shooters Hill Road (Chesterfield Walk)

Cross over Crooms Hill opposite the entrance to the Manor House and walk south towards Shooters Hill Road along Chesterfield Walk ignoring initially the old roadway and footpath into Greenwich Park.

The property at the top of Crooms Hill on the east side and just before the above track to the Park is the **White House,** which is of ancient interest but the present structure is more likely to represent a late 18th century rebuilding. Like **Hillside**, to its north, it does not stand on Heath waste, unlike the magnificent Manor House, opposite. However, Chesterfield Walk,

named after Lord Chesterfield, who was resident at what we now call Rangers House from 1748 to 1773, was an encroachment on the Heath made in the late 17th century on an agreement of 1688 between Andrew Snape and the Crown.

Three houses were built on the ground but only one now survives: **Macartney House** (the name dates from 1795, when it was owned by descendants of the Macartneys of Auchinleck). This is a gathering of buildings, partly once the homes of the Stanley family, the Earls of Derby. One famous resident was Lt Col Edward Wolfe (d1759), father of General Sir James Wolfe (1727-1759), the hero of Quebec. For over 350 years it was a Crown property and was converted into flats in 1926-1927.

Rangers House with bund and posts along the A2 in 2010

The next house along Chesterfield Walk is **Rangers House**, built in 1699-1700 by and for Vice Admiral Francis Hosier (1673-1727), Admiral of the Blue Squadron. He spent much time away at sea and succumbed to yellow fever in Portobello. Subsequent residents included Philip Dormer Stanhope, 4th Earl of Chesterfield (1694-1773). He authorised the extension to the south side of the House for his picture gallery. In 1815 the house became the formal grace and favour residence for the Ranger of Greenwich Park (an office of honour with no profit or duties) in which it remained, mostly, until the last resident Ranger – Field Marshal Garnet Wolseley (1833-1913) moved out in 1896. In 1899 the Crown sold it to the

London County Council, who sub-let it in part for use as a refreshment room for visitors to Greenwich Park and Blackheath. Rangers House was restored by the GLC in 1960 and in 1974 designated as an Historic House Museum in which to display a fine collection of Tudor portraits, attributed to William Larkin (c1580-1619). These are now at Kenwood, in Hampstead, and Rangers House (since the abolition of the GLC) is in the custody of English Heritage. It houses the art collection and furniture of diamond merchant Sir Julius Charles Wernher (1850-1912), which he left to the Nation. At the time of printing the house was open only on a restricted basis.

By about 1903, lawn tennis was played on the horseshoe green in front of Rangers House but the tennis players retreated to a court on the site of Montague House, behind the south-west corner of the Greenwich Park wall (*see below*). **Lawn bowls** had taken off, so to speak, in the late 19th century, when it was planned by the Blackheath and Greenwich Bowling Cub to lay down a green between the Blackheath Brewery, in Blackheath

Cricket in front of Rangers House c. 1840

Vale, and Talbot Place [see Central Walk]. But the local residents would have none of it so the green was put down close to Rangers House in July 1903. The BGBC moved to Brooklands Park in April 1926 and others took over a re-laid green on the Heath.

Beyond Rangers House fixed to the wall are two distinctive marks: the first indicates the exact line of the **0 deg. meridian** and the other is a plaque marking the ceremony in 1977, when HM Queen Elizabeth II planted the first of an avenue of lime trees to replace the previous grove, probably not for the first time.

The corner of the Park Wall, where Chesterfield Walk, Shooters Hill Road and Charlton Way meet, was known as Mole's Corner, a corruption of one George Moult, a brewer, who built a small house of distinctive style with a conical tower, which sat on the wall. It was later extended and incorporated into the grounds of a house called **Montague House**, built for Ralph, the Earl of Montague (d1709) in 1702. It absorbed Moult's House in 1717. At the very end of the 18th century Montague House was taken as a residence for HRH Caroline of Brunswick, Princess of Wales (1768-1821), on her estrangement from the HRH Prince of Wales (1762-1830) later George IV. Caroline lived here until about 1812, using the garden ground across the Heath and a pavilion called **The Pagoda** (see above).

West elevation of Montague House by J. Smith in 1755

Montague House was demolished in 1815, some said because of the Prince of Wales' hostility towards his spouse. The space for the house is now taken up by public tennis courts. In the Park there is a tiled plunge pool known as "Queen Caroline's Bath", although she was never crowned as such. The foundations for the house are lost under the tennis court tight into the corner of the south-west corner of Greenwich Park. Traces of the fenestration can be seen on the Park side of the boundary wall.

History Section 9: Chesterfield Walk to the Blackheath Gate

Turn left (east) at the end of Chesterfield Walk and follow the Greenwich Park Wall along Charlton Way until you come to the Blackheath Gate, which is the main southern entrance to the Park. This is the end of the West Walk, but you could continue with the East Walk or turn south and walk along Duke Humphrey Road and back to Blackheath Village (see also the Central Walk in reverse direction).

The first building you will see on the Heath and opposite the Park Wall is the **Heath Keeper's House** or Metropolitan Lodge, when first built by the Metropolitan Board of Works in 1882. It was to provide a home for the Heath manager, and remained so until 1991 when the last

Heath Keeper's House c. 1910

resident Keeper, Mr Roy Fox, retired. Since then it has fallen empty and derelict. It was repaired and partially restored by the local authority in 2003 for a public servant, but not for a Heath manager. You will then see the abandoned public lavatories, built in 1896, but closed for a lack of funding (for supervision and maintenance one supposes) by the local authority.

Next you will come to the **Folly Pond**, scraped out of a gravel pit by the Board of Works. The original scheme had been to create a five acre lake in the Crown Pit (Circus Field) to help ease unemployment. Instead, a smaller pit was taken and in 1886-87 the Folly Pond was created, with two small islands. Mature trees were planted all round and it was much

appreciated especially when the LCC decided in August 1922 to make it a children's boating pond with child-sized rowing and paddle boats, with a man in a hut to take the money and shout the numbers of the rowers

Folly Pond c. 1930

who stayed out too long. This activity stopped in 1939 and was not revived, although when frozen over the pond was attractive to skaters. In the 1980s the basin of the pond was damaged and it dried out and cracked. Repairs and a water supply ensured that this would, hopefully, be prevented in future. The big storm of 1987 took down a number of the original trees, by then well matured and of considerable size.

Just outside the gates to the Park and on the Heath is the **donkey ride** – by tradition a stand for donkeys and ponies let out at fair time since the 1830s, but in more recent years every weekend in the summer. Unfortunately, however, with the death of the donkey man, Len Thorne, in 2012, there is some doubt over whether this venerable tradition will be continued. Originally, there were cobble donkey rides both sides of the road – perhaps one was for ponies. Mangers were fixed to the protective post and rails; originally, there were two drinking troughs at the Shooters Hill Road end of the walks, provided for any passing animal, not just donkeys and ponies. The north stub of Duke Humphrey Road, which survives, was taken over by ice cream sellers and questionable coach parking. A drinking fountain once stood on the north-east corner of Duke Humphrey Road and Charlton Way, but had been removed by Edwardian times.

West Walk Summary

Road	Building/Feature	Map No.	His. Sec.
Tranquil Vale, Blackheath Village	Start of West Walk		1
Lloyds Place	Eastnor House	62	1
Grotes Building	Nos 3, 6	103	1
	Nos 19-26, Eliot Place	104	
Grotes Place	No 1		1
	No 2 (Canister House)		
Hare and Billet Road	Hare and Billet Pub.	58	
	Hare and Billet Pond	57	
	Site of Marr's Ravine		
Eliot Place	Nos (14, 15,) 9, 6	42, 41	2
	No 2 (Blue Plaque)		
	No 1 (Heathfield House)	40	
Eliot Vale (a short cut)	Nos 8, 9	39	2
	The Close (West Lodge)	105	
	Heath Lane		
Orchard Drive	North Several	107	2
The Orchard	Lynn Court (Orchard House)	24	3
Aberdeen Terrace	Nos 7-8 (ex-NUPE)	108	3
	The Pagoda	23	
	Nos 1-6 Eliot Vale	106	
Mounts Pond Road	Granville House etc.	109	3
	The Old Knoll	22	
Eliot Hill	Eliot Pits		3
	The Hermitage	20	
	Nos 7-12 (Eliot Lodge)	21	
Wat Tyler Road	Greyladies Gardens (Holly Hedge House)	110 17	4
	Dartmouth Court	111	
	Lydia/Sherwell Houses	112	

Road	Building/Feature	Map No.	His. Sec.
Dartmouth Terrace	Dartmouth Field (Green Man Hotel) Cross A2 at lights	11	4
The Point	Viewpoint	2	5
	Disused chalk caverns	1	
	RAF pilot memorial	2	
West Grove	No 18 (Point House)	4	6
	No 14 (The Crosslets)	5	
	Nos 3, 4 (Chocolate Hse)	6	
	Conduit head	7	
	Cross over Hyde Vale		
West Grove Lane (a diversion)	West Grove House	113	6
	West Grove Terrace	114	
Cade Road	Fountain, horse trough	10, 9	7
	Views (just)		
Crooms Hill	Manor House	28	7
	Chesterfield Gardens.	115	
	St. Ursula's School	116	
Chesterfield Walk	Hillside	25	8
	White House	27	
	McCartney House	30	
	Rangers House	33	
	Lawn bowls	31	
	0 deg. Meridian	117	
	Courts (Montague Hse)	34	
Charlton Way	Heath Keeper's House	43	9
	Folly Pond	46	
	Donkey Ride	47	
	Blackheath Gates	45	
	Finish of West Walk		

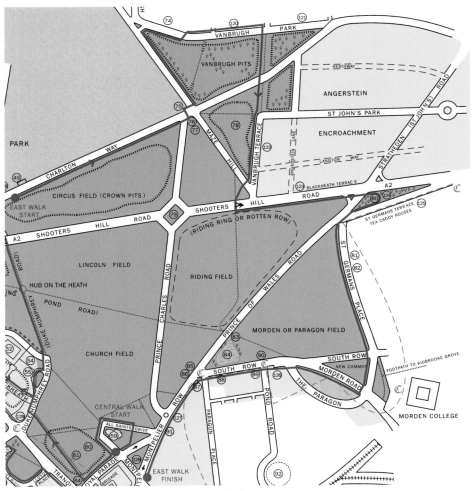

2. The East Walk

History Section 10: Blackheath Gates of Greenwich Park to Maze Hill

Start of Walk at the Blackheath Gates to Greenwich Park

Start this walk at the Blackheath Gate, which is the main southern entrance to Greenwich Park and, after you have studied its fine proportions, walk east along Charlton Way to the traffic lights at Maze Hill.

The southern entrance to the Park was once a simple wooden gate opened only during the Bank Holidays for the huge crowds which descended on the Heath and Greenwich Park. But in 1855 a handsome set of iron gates and gate piers were erected – widened slightly in 1901-1902 with dedicated entrances for cyclists. These were taken away for the 2012 Olympics, but after the event the bricks were cleaned and the piers reassembled four yards further back along with their original lamps. The gates were also widened to allow larger vehicles an easier turn into the park from Charlton Way.

This is one of the most interesting sections of the walk, although it might seem unpromising, except to students of 17th century brickwork, with a long plain section of **Greenwich Park Wall**. Notwithstanding, the prospect across the Heath which encompasses the view from the east (far left towards Kidbrooke) to the west (far right to Dartmouth terrace) is spectacular and takes in all the important points.

The 12-foot Park Wall dates (in part) from 1616-1624, when it replaced a simple security fence although much has been rebuilt over the centuries. There is little of interest on the wall except close to the Blackheath Gates where a memorial **plaque** names the leaders and marks the 500th anniversary of the Cornish rebellion and the Battle of Blackheath Field, of 1497. The plaque erected by the London Cornish Association and the Cornish Gorsedd is in English and Cornish and was unveiled on 21 June 1997.

To the south side of Charlton Way is the space always known these days as Circus Field, but in earlier times as the Crown Pits. The latter name almost certainly came because the ground here had been dug for gravel, probably illegally. In time the digging created a deep and wide pit – similar to the Vanbrugh and Eliot Pits, sometimes with a small pond in the middle, possibly fed by a spring, although this was drained and closed over in 1827, much to the regret of the drovers. It was ground much used for activities and assemblies. Evidence of land springs was visible until the mid 19th century on the north-east corner of the field, next to the Gibb Memorial.

Once the Heath funfairs and informal markets had been established in the early 19th century, the showmen took over and many of the entertainments and refreshment booths were placed in the pits below ground level. This continued until 1939-1945 but after the war ended the pits were filled in with bomb rubble and levelled over with thin topsoil. The funfairs and circuses continued thereafter and the former caused considerable damage to the grass surface in the 1970s and 1980s. The funfairs these days are fewer than before and less widespread. Greenwich Council does, from time to time, let the Circus Field for circuses, as also does Lewisham Council on the Old Donkey Field on the other side of the A2.

Circus Field and A2 c.1905

all round the field and planted with wild flower mixes and poppies. There are three dedicated entrances; the principal one is on Prince Charles Road north of Camomile Bottom and the other two along Charlton Way. All three have low level gates, which are only opened for fairground or circus use.

At the corner of Charlton Way with Maze Hill at the traffic lights is the **War Memorial**. It was erected by the Borough Council in 1922 to commemorate the 1,600 dead and wounded from Greenwich in the Great War (1914-1918) – and subsequently updated to include the World War of 1939-1945. Dedicated on 11 November 1922 and unveiled by Greenwich solicitor Harry Bolton Sewell (1859-1941), whose son, Lt Cecil Harold Sewell VC (*post*), was killed in action in August 1918, aged but 23.

Also note the **Gibb Memorial** Drinking Fountain, clock and shelter on the south-eastern side of the traffic lights. It was erected as a memorial to Greenwich Alderman and benefactor Andrew Gibb (1853-1908), the cost

Circus Field and A2 for London Olympics, 2012

Gibb and War Memorials off Maze Hill in 2009

During the 2012 Olympics the ground was taken as an overflow and logistics centre for the Equestrian events for both the Olympics and Paralympics. By the time this book is in circulation evidence of damage to the surface may still be apparent. One attempt to prevent illegal parking has been the raising of bunds – two foot high boundary humps

being met from the estate of his widow, Isabella (1848-1926). While it survived well over many decades, hooligans damaged it almost beyond repair in the 1980s and 1990s. It was restored in 2003, although without a water supply, many authorities contributing handsomely towards the cost. It was unveiled by Mrs Janet Gilman, then Mayor of Greenwich in November 2003.

You can now walk north along Maze Hill and turn right into Vanbrugh Park opposite the small gate into Greenwich Park. Continue along this road until you see Vanbrugh Park Road on your left; turn right here along the footpath between the Vanbrugh Pits, cross over Charlton Way and this leads you into Vanbrugh Terrace, which is notable for its eight fine houses. At the southern end of this road is the pedestrian crossing of Shooters Hill Road.

At some stage here you should certainly take the opportunity to walk freely over the old gravel diggings known as the Vanbrugh Pits, which are some of the wildest and most attractive sections of the entire Heath.

Beyond the edge of the Heath on the far north-west corner is the **Vanbrugh triangle** on which, from 1718, architect playwright Sir John Vanbrugh (1664-1726) put his own home, Vanbrugh Castle, in 1719, and a number of other distinctive dwellings (all since demolished) for his family. His lease from Sir Michael Biddulph (d1719) stretched south to the corner of what is now Vanbrugh Park. In the mid 1920s much of the triangle was taken for a new Roan Foundation secondary school for boys. It was designed by Percy Boothroyd Dannatt (1879-1968) and Sir Banister Flight Fletcher (1866-1953) and opened by the then Minister of Education in March 1928. On the north frontage of the

The opening of the Drill House, Vanbrugh Park, in 1862

Heath is the great stretch of Vanbrugh Park from Nos 1 to 27. Before that, at the west end, stood a drill hall designed by Alfred Gilbert (1826-1873) for the West Kent Rifle Volunteers in 1861. It ended its life as a furniture store but was destroyed by fire in 1951 and its site and that of Nos 1-5 Vanbrugh Park developed for the **Parkside** flats in the early 1960s. Nos 6 to 14 were partly damaged in the war but all were demolished for the **municipal estate** designed by architects Chamberlain, Powell & Bon in 1965. The group from **No 15**

Nos. 7-15 Vanbrugh Park in 1905 - only no.15 (on the right) survives

(Elgin Lodge) to No 26 survive today. **No 27** (Westcombe House) was built for James Kollé Soames (1850-1915), soap and candle maker whose family firm was set on the Greenwich Peninsula. It is now the senior department of the **Blackheath High School for Girls**.

All this faces south to the Vanbrugh Pits, the scars and hollows created by gravel digging for building works which took place on the Heath from earliest time until the mid 19th century. The last extraction was for building the Vanbrugh Estate in 1870. Thereafter, the much-scarred land was taken over by gorse.

After gravel digging was forbidden by the Board of Works the Pits became a playground for local children. The Board's surveyors eased the sides of the deepest pits and installed the steps on both edges of the large pit and, as the top soil improved by the 1920s, the trees and shrubberies grew up and thickened, there was a substantial increase in the ecological quality of this land, especially since the late 1950s. The sylvicultural quality of the Vanbrugh Pits was not always without attendant risk because of the misuse of the hollows by cyclists, tobogganers, other sporting amateurs and arsonists. Nevertheless, trees do flourish in the 21st century and the following specimens have been noted: oak, ash, birch, lime, and many shrubs. [*See also the Introduction paragraphs on ecology*]

History Section 12: Vanbrugh Terrace to St Germans Place

Cross over the A2 at the pedestrian lights at the end of Vanbrugh Terrace and walk east on the Heath following the line of Shooters Hill Road until you come to the traffic lights. To see the ancient milestone (six miles to London and nine miles to Dartford) you will need to cross Prince of Wales Road here and look near the base of the pedestrian lights for crossing Shooters Hill Road. The "Tea Caddy Houses" are on the south side of the road at this point.

Although John Julius Angerstein (1735-1823) enclosed 11 hectares (26 plus acres) of Blackheath, which he regarded as rubbish strewn waste, the gravel pit to the west, opposite Vanbrugh Terrace, was not part of his

This pit in front of Vanbrugh Terrace held a barrage balloon in WW2

enclosure. During the 1939-1945 war it housed a barrage balloon which could be tethered within the pit, fully inflated. It was filled in with bomb rubble in 1945 and the surface grassed over.

Despite enclosing a large chunk of the Heath, the northern boundary now marked by Vanbrugh Park and the west end of Vanbrugh Terrace, there was no development of this land until 1839. In that year the Angerstein trustees granted building licences to a variety of Blackheath tradesmen for what became Blackheath Terrace (Nos 7-33 Shooters Hill Road). These houses, 14 houses in seven semi-detached pairs, were designed in a distinctive Palladian style, and are erroneously called the **"Captains' Houses"** because it has been claimed that they were built as a present

for Nelson's 14 Captains who served with him at the Battle of Trafalgar (1805). This story was clearly rubbish and it has been admitted, by the perpetrator, that it was a 1960s joke by one of the residents which local estate agents picked up and carried on.

It is possible that the designer for the Blackheath Terrace houses was Greenwich town centre and Trafalgar Tavern architect Joseph Kay (1775-1847), but the evidence is circumstantial.

The section of Shooters Hill Road at its junction with Vanbrugh Terrace is the site of the start for the elite runners in the annual London Marathon, which usually occurs towards the end of April.

The start of the London Marathon 2010

There was a secondary development over a large rectangle on the corner of Shooters Hill Road which took the name Vanbrugh Terrace in 1853, designed by architects Robert Richardson Banks (1813-1872) and Charles Barry (1823-1900); the plot also gave space for Nos 1, 3 and 5 Shooters Hill Road. No 1 (Heath House) dates from 1853.

No 35 and No 37, on opposite Stratheden Road corners, were both doctors' houses for many decades and known locally as Scylla & Charybdis. Opposite No 37 and the petrol station (open in 1932) and just across the road is the **milestone** marking the distances to Charing Cross and Dartford.

The slim triangle of land beyond is part of the Heath and was once considered for a children's playground. The tree planting (modern)

Milestone and Tea Caddy Houses in 1983

has been cultivated to create a sound baffle between the "**Tea Caddy Houses**" (Nos 2-20 Shooters Hill Road) and the main Shooters Hill trunk road (A2), despite the terms of the Blackheath Act of 1871, which forbids the planting of trees on the Heath.

History Section 13: St Germans Place to Morden Road

After admiring the "Tea Caddy Houses", walk south along St Germans Place, cross over Kidbrooke Gardens and note the fine entrance and driveway up to Morden College.

The Heath in this area was renowned for its sports in the past, but today (since 1990) large parts are left uncut and boast mature summer meadows with plentiful wild flowers and grasses. It provides some of the most attractive prospects or views over the old **Riding Ring** and **Morden** (or **Paragon**) **Field**.

The highways Shooters Hill Road, Prince of Wales Road and Prince Charles Road encompass the ground which was laid down as a legal

riding field in the 1870s. Horse riding on public parks was usually forbidden because of the damage done to the grass and turf by horse shoes, especially if ridden frequently.

The Board of Works decided in 1872 that Blackheath was a suitable place for a riding ring or rotten row - a large ring of oiled sand - and the Blackheath version was opened in 1873 and known in official parlance as the Riding Field. It was hugely popular but the Great War of 1914-1918 reduced its use by local riding stables and in 1918 it was formally closed for lack of interest. The last remnants disappeared when the field was subject to repair and re-levelling. Because there were few stables in the vicinity – by 1939 only one - there was little evidence of public regret. It was only when it had gone that people started to grumble at its loss. Yet the Hyde Park Rotten Row, which dates from about the 1850s, survives today.

The King's Troop in front of Riding Field in 2013

An echo of this equestrian tradition can be seen occasionally today when the King's Troop of the Royal Horse Artillery, stationed at Woolwich, exercise some of its 111 horses on the roads across the Heath.

The Morden and/or Paragon Fields enjoy significance as a sporting field because of the proximity of buildings once in school use. St Germans Place, which sprang up in the years 1820-1830, boasted a proprietary chapel. It was later embraced as St Germans Chapel by the local diocese (Southwark).

The Chapel had been built to provide spiritual education to its neighbouring school for boys, opened in 1823 by Rev William Greenlaw (1781-1850). Services at the chapel were taken either by William or by his brother the Rev Richard Bathurst Greenlaw (1794-1855).

The school flourished through the 19th century, eventually passing to the Rev Frederick Wilkins Aveling (1851-1937), related through marriage to Eleanor, daughter of philosopher Karl Marx (1818-1883). Aveling renamed the Blackheath enterprise Christ's College in 1894, after the school in Taunton where he was employed previously. He conducted his Blackheath school on Christian Socialist principles. The College is now **The Blackheath Preparatory School** (since 1996) and has a co-educational intake aged between 3 and 11 years. It has retained the coat of arms of the Taunton enterprise.

St Germans Place School and Chapel in 1832 by John Gilbert

The **Chapel** survived with a supportive congregation until the 1939-1945 war, when it was bomb-damaged. Diocesan promises of repair were abandoned because of falling support and it was sold off for development to developers Messrs Wates. The site is now occupied by No 5a-5e St Germans Place, designed in 1969 by architect Lorenzo Mansini.

None of this disturbed the use of the Heath for games, in particular cricket: an 1832 drawing by John Gilbert indicates this clearly. The schools played here and so did the best local teams: the Morden and the Paragon cricket clubs. They merged interests in 1885 to create the Blackheath Cricket Club and the team moved with the footballers off the Heath to the Rectory Field, on Charlton Road, shortly afterwards. The exigencies of the 1939-1945 war led to the erection of two rows of prefabricated houses ("prefabs") on the Heath along St Germans Place in October 1945. Similar groups appeared at Mounts Pond Road and Talbot Place.

St Germans Place with prefabs. in the 1950s

At the very end of St Germans Place is the small triangle of Heath known in the late 17th century as the New Common. It leads to the entrance to **Morden College**, a refuge for Christian Turkey Company merchants down on their luck through no fault of their own, which was established by Sir John Morden in 1695. The Travers' survey notes it in 1695-96 as "*Sir John Morden's New Hospital*". It opened early in 1700, designed by Christopher Wren's master mason, Edward Strong (1652-1724). The College, one of Blackheath's finest buildings, has remained providing

Morden College in c.1905

shelter to the elderly ever since, although it now takes both sexes and its estate has been considerably enlarged since the distinctive Wren-style quad was erected.

To the north of the entrance to the College is Kidbrooke Gardens. This road did not exist until 1904 when a large house, Kidbrooke Lodge, was demolished and its ground cleared for Kidbrooke Gardens and Liskeard Gardens, the opportunity taken then to cut a new road from the Heath to Kidbrooke Grove and on to Kidbrooke Park Road. To the south is an ancient public footpath leading to the same destination, from which you can see other Morden College buildings.

History Section 14: Morden Road and South Row to Blackheath Village

After studying the front of Morden College turn west along Morden Road and South Row. This will give you initially a fine view of the Paragon, particularly if the trees are not in leaf.

At the end of South Row the thirsty walker may like to call in at the Princess of Wales public house; if not, he/she should continue in a westerly direction along Montpelier Row, past the Clarendon Hotel to Blackheath Village, which is the end of the East Walk. If you have the energy you may wish to take the Central Walk back to your start at the Blackheath Gates of Greenwich Park or the even longer west walk to the same destination. Otherwise there is a plethora of buses and trains in the Village to many destinations.

Built over the years 1793 to 1805, the 14 house crescent of **The Paragon** was designed by architect Michael Searles (1751-1813). In 1793 the Greenwich vestry, spotting a chance of a new supply of rates for the Parish coffers, had placed a **boundary stone** on its corner close to **Paragon House** (of 1791) although some of the site did fall within the Lewisham manor. The Paragon complex was badly damaged in the 1939-1945 war but fully restored by architect Charles Bernard Brown (1910-1990) as flats behind the original façade.

The Paragon, like its close neighbour Morden College, is one of the most outstanding architectural compositions in the country let alone London. Despite the alterations brought about by war damage the crescent

The Paragon after war damage

is statutorily listed Grade I, and has become one of the most popular architectural sites sought out by tourists to Blackheath and Greenwich. Local people enjoy a pardonable pride that the Paragon is part of their landscape.

When built, the Paragon was split between the parishes of Greenwich and Lewisham – the boundary passing through No 7. In 1900 the local authorities agreed this was not sensible and Nos 1-14 The Paragon and No 1 South Row (Paragon House) were formally transferred to the Greenwich local authority. The remainder of South Row stayed with Lewisham.

The green to the front of the Paragon was judged not to be part of the waste of Blackheath and was separated from the Heath by a controversial hedge and ditch, marked as a ha-ha on an 1847 surveyor's plan. However, landscaping pedants often fail to categorize it in this way. In 1931 the half circle front lawn was protected by the London Squares Preservation Act.

To the west of the Paragon was a line of plain houses called **South Row** in one of which (No 3) was a famous school conducted by "Felix" (Nicholas Wanostrocht [1804-1876]), the finest cricketer of his time. His pupils were encouraged to play cricket on the Morden/Paragon field to the detriment of their lessons and Wanostrocht's school went bankrupt in the 1840s.

South Row was badly damaged in 1941 and its ruins demolished. It was replaced in 1962-63 by the present **Span Estate**, an important

South Row now replaced by a Span Estate

contemporary group of buildings (now listed Grade II) and designed by architect Eric Lyons (1912-1980). A major historic survivor at the west end is the 1804 **Colonnade House**, with its original limestone, and now listed, gate piers. This was also designed by Michael Searles, architect of the Paragon and No 20 Montpelier Row (*see below*).

Opposite South Row is the **Prince of Wales boating pond**, now largely given over to water fowl, with a distinctive duck house tethered in its centre; it became a favourite gathering place for

Prince of Wales Pond in c.1905

families to picnic. There was a drover's pond here in the 17th century, fed by an underground stream leading from a spring in Greenwich Park. In the 1720s the Pond was reconstructed into a large rectangle and deepened to provide a head of water for the fountains and water supply to the grand Palladian house of Wricklemarsh Park, about 500 yards to the south. This palatial mansion, which dominated Blackheath from the south side of the Heath to as far away as Lee Green, was designed by architect John James (1672-1746) for Sir Gregory Page (1689-1775), one of the richest men in England. The house was demolished in the years 1787-1799. Pond Road marks its north carriageway.

With the demolition of **Wricklemarsh House** in the 1790s the pond reverted to a wild state, largely used for watering horses and cattle, the edges worn down. When the Board of Works took over in 1871 it was remade into the shape we see today, concrete-lined and designed to be suitable for model boats, with a shaped cobbled entrance slope to the north edge for the benefit of horses and carts. Even so, when the boating pond froze hard enough it was a popular destination for skaters until recent years.

The South East Model Yacht club adopted it as its "official" pond in 1908, but the London County Council refused a request to give it exclusive rights. In the last 10 years or so the ducks and geese have taken over although the boating enthusiasts still retain a hold, gathering for special boating days from time to time. The pond takes its name from the Prince of Wales road close by and not from the adjacent pub.

Princess of Wales Hotel and Tavern

The Princess of Wales public house (with an address in Montpelier Row) was in business with that name by 1808, and its sign was a tribute to mark the residence in Blackheath of HRH Princess Caroline Elisabeth of Brunswick-Wolfenbuttel (1768-1821), consort to the Prince Regent, later George IV (1762-1830). The Board of Works tried to prevent a landlord erecting a **sign** to his pub on the Heath. Although he retained it by arguing successfully that it was there before the Metropolitan Board of Works came on the scene and that the pub had acquired prescriptive rights – something not possible on the north side of the Heath, because that part is Crown land.

Part of the ground on which the Paragon and South Row were built was included as manorial waste, on the open Heath, in a 1696 survey, along with the triangular field fronted on the west side by Montpelier Row, and now encompassed by Paragon Place and Wemyss Road. In the time of the 2nd Earl of Dartmouth, it was let on a 1,000 year lease to Gregory Page, who enclosed this land in the 1720s within his Wricklemarsh Park. Timber merchant John Cator (1728-1806), purchaser of the Wricklemarsh Estate in 1783, bought the freehold and developed it during 1795-1805 for the present houses in Montpelier Row.

The landmark feature these days for the Row is the **Clarendon Hotel**, originally Nos 8-16 Montpelier Row, merchant's houses in the late 18th century, which had passed largely into hotel and boarding house use soon after the 1914-1918 war. Architectural history enthusiasts should note **No 20 (The Square House**, of 1803, by Michael Searles (the Paragon architect) and **No 19**, **Alverstoke House** by architect and District Surveyor Benjamin Tabberer (1831-1910) in 1885. **Nos 23 and 24** (once St Christopher's House, a college for training Sunday school teachers) were built originally as a pair of semi-detached houses in 1792. They were linked and extended sideways and upwards for a school in the 1860s; the block became a branch of the YWCA from 1916 to 1962 and now is in small flats.

Finally, for this section of the Heath walk strollers may regret the loss of the **gentlemen's lavatory**, installed in the Heath opposite No 5 Montpelier Row in October 1900, to relieve the nuisance caused by the crowds attracted to the Princess of Wales public house on Saturday nights. For some reason it was removed in the 1960s.

The walker will now be close to the Village, and can note as he (or she) goes the battered public notice board and the horse trough at the south end of Montpelier Row. It enjoys no inscription, alas, but is of rough and ready concrete so any wording may have weathered away. This may be a modern installation designed for horticulture rather than equestrian relief.

No longer used by horses (if it ever was) it provides a suitable container for an attractive floral display. The troughs were originally at Downham, but Lewisham Council moved one to Royal Parade and another to its present position.

On occasions a Christmas tree might appear on a small triangle of grass, with bench and trees, on what has been recently named as **Phoenix Field**, after the name for the north-east section of Blackheath Village. The element of Montpelier Vale facing the Heath was once Nos 1-6 Royal Parade. In 1903 the shops here were the first to enjoy electric street lighting in the district and were known (albeit briefly) as Electric Parade. It was later incorporated into the numbering of Montpelier Vale. Royal Parade (*see Central Walk*) carried on minus its Numbers 1-6.

Montpelier Row with the Heath's Green Flag awarded again in 2013

East Walk Summary

Road	Building/Feature	Map No.	His. Sec.
Blackheath Gates, Charlton Way	Start of East Walk	45	10
	Cornish Plaque	118	
	War Memorial	75	
	Gibb Memorial	76	
	Circus Field (funfairs)		
Maze Hill	Park wall		11
Vanbrugh Park	Top of Vanbrugh triangle	119	11
	Parkside flats (Drill House)	74	
	Municipal estate (nos 6-14)	120	
	Nos 15-27	121	
	Vanbrugh Pits		
Vanbrugh Terrace	Nos 1-8	122	11
	Cross A2 at lights		
Shooters Hill Road	'Captains' Houses'	123	12
	Milestone	124	
	'Tea Caddy Houses'	125	
St. Germans Place	Riding Field		13
	Paragon/Morden Field		
	Blackheath Prep. School	81	
	5 a-e (site of Chapel)	82	
	Morden College		
Morden Road	The Paragon		14
South Row	Boundary stone	90	14
	Paragon House	126	
	Span Estate (site of no 3)	89	
	Colonnade House	88	
	Prince of Wales Pond	84	
	(Wricklemarsh House)	102	
Montpelier Row	Princess of Wales Pub.	87	14
	Pub. sign on Heath	85	
	Clarendon Hotel	127	
	No 19, Alverstoke House		
	No 20, Square House	91	
	Nos 23, 24		
	(Underground lavatories)	86	
	Phoenix Field	128	
	Finish of East Walk		

BLACKHEATH.

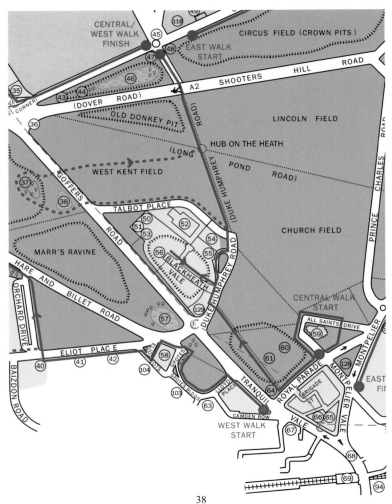

CENTRAL/
WEST WALK
FINISH

45
118

49

CIRCUS FIELD (CROWN PITS)

48
47
EAST WALK
START

35
46

43 44

A2   SHOOTERS   HILL   ROAD

(DOVER   ROAD)

S CORNER

OLD DONKEY PIT

36

LINCOLN   FIELD

HUB ON THE HEATH

(LONG   POND   ROAD)

WEST KENT FIELD

(DUKE HUMPHREY   ROAD)

37

GOFFERS

38

ROAD

TALBOT PLACE

CHURCH   FIELD

PRINCE   CHARLES   ROAD

50

MARR'S RAVINE

51

52

53

54

56

55

BLACKHEATH
VALE

HARE   AND   BILLET   ROAD

DUKE HUMPHREY ROAD

CENTRAL WALK
START

ALL SAINTS DRIVE

129

ORCHARD DRIVE

57

59

60

ELIOT   PLACE

58

61

128

MONTPELIER

EAST
FI

40

41

42

104

TRANQUIL

64

ROYAL PARADE

BAIZDON ROAD

103

GROTES

LLOYD
PLACE

GROTES BLDGS

BRIGADE

MONTPELIER VALE

63

65

CAMDEN ROW

66

68

WEST WALK
START

VALE

67

69

94

3: The Central Walk

History Section 15: Royal Parade to Duke Humphrey Road

Start of Walk at Royal Parade

The Central Walk starts in Royal Parade at the top, northern end of Blackheath Village, where you will see All Saints' Church immediately in front of you. You can easily do a circuit of the church before heading across the grass in a westerly direction parallel to Royal Parade to see the Victorian drinking fountain at the corner with Tranquil Vale. Turn right here along the footpath with a gentle upward slope across the Heath until you meet Duke Humphrey Road.

The Village triangle of Montpelier Vale, Tranquil Vale and Royal Parade was an enclosure of a part of the Heath in the late 18th/early 19th century. Initially, it was occupied by the site of the Village well – the **Queen Elizabeth Well**, on the south side of Tranquil Passage and now hidden under the floor of **Tranquil Hall** (built 1851 as the Village school). In 1724 Sir Gregory Page *(see Wricklemarsh, above)* decided to get rid of the handful of houses and buildings on the west side of his Park – roughly where Blackheath Grove and Wemyss Road are now. The ancient pub – the Three Tuns, once close to what is now Barclay's Bank - was a going concern and the landlord, Richardson Headly, came to an agreement with the Dartmouth estate to move his house to Tranquil Vale, close

to the well. It kept its original name and has been situated there ever since although rebuilt in 1883 as it appears today. Alas, the pub owners decided that the 300 year old name was not relevant to modern trading practice so, to the horror of the community, decided to rebrand it as an "Irish" pub and call it "**O'Neill's**".

The location of the well and the pub soon attracted other buildings to the waste and, with Dartmouth approval, was quickly covered with houses and commercial premises during the decades 1790-1810.

The growing village of Blackheath had long needed an established Anglican place of worship nearer than St Margaret's, Lee. The first choice for a site (the gift of the Earl of Dartmouth) was a triangle near the Hare & Billet public house, but the neighbours objected. So it was decided that an open plot, on the Heath, despite it being an encroachment on the commoners' rights, would be chosen. As it happens the decision was a good one and the location seems to hold the corner of the Heath and the Village triangle together as the centre of the community.

All Saints' Church 1857

All Saints' Church was designed in the Gothic Revival style by architect Benjamin Ferry (1810-1880) and opened for worship on All Saints' Day in November 1858. The three main blocks, in Kentish ragstone, were ready then, but it took until 1867-68 to add the steeple and vestry. The west end porch was added in 1898-99 and was designed by Sir Arthur Blomfield (1828-1899). The protective circle of iron railings was lost for the scrap metal drive during the 1939-1945 war, and not replaced thereafter. The floodlighting dates from 2002.

The Village traders gave a demonstration of their loyalty to mark HM Queen Victoria's Diamond Jubilee in 1897 with the placing of an ornate **drinking fountain** on the Heath at the west end of Royal Parade. It has to be said that the traders failed their fund raising target by quite an amount and well-wishers (including the LCC) had to make up the balance. The

Royal Parade with Drinking Fountain in 1897

inscription has weathered since and, like the other fountains around the Heath, there is no water to be had for either dog or man.

The footpath you follow across the Heath is across the infilled **Washerwomen's Field (or Bottom)**, once a shallow gravel pit and known as Gilbert's Piece in 1695. The ground was much trenched in preparations for the 1939-1945 war and was filled with bomb rubble in 1944/45 and levelled.

It took its early 19th century name from the proximity of Washerwomen's Row, a string of small cottages largely occupied by launderers and allied trades. By tradition they dried their customers' clothing and bed sheets on the gorse bushes in the pit opposite their houses. The cottages were lost for Royal Parade in 1863-65. Nevertheless, local laundresses continued to use the Heath for drying but the London County Council abolished the right in 1893 by granting just three annual licences, to expire in 1894. Their place had been taken, to some extent, in January 1891, by an LCC organised quoits ground, close to All Saints' Church, managed on a first-come first-served basis.

A few trees were planted (against custom and practice for the Heath) to mark the 1871-1971 centenary and, despite the odds, they have flourished and the field here is popular for picnic parties seeking shade. In the 1980s an attempt by an eager restaurateur to place tables and chairs on the Heath was quickly frustrated.

History Section 16: Duke Humphrey Road to Talbot Place

When you reach Duke Humphrey Road note the four-storey block of flats immediately in front of you, which is Goffers House; turn right here and then into Blackheath Vale on your left after 30 yards. This is a cul-de-sac so when you have explored it continue north along Duke Humphrey Road following the house frontages.

On the site of what is now **Goffers House** and looking at the Village was originally a nine-cottage group called Union Vale. It was sited halfway down the incline into the old sand pit (*see below*) so that its front garden ground sloped up to the edge of the public roadway. The rear of the site, in the western slope of Blackheath Vale was refilled in the 1950s by municipal houses after war damage in 1944. This was largely on the site of stables and workshops, some of which had been in place by the late 18th century. Union Vale had been demolished for a more upmarket group of four villas: Talbot Houses (Talbot being a Dartmouth family name: Lord Talbot's daughter, Lady Frances, was the first wife of the 4th Earl

Talbot Houses in 1938 - now Goffers House

of Dartmouth). The two pairs of semi-detached houses were completed in the late 1870s. Two were badly damaged by a Flying Bomb (V1) in July 1944, and the whole site was eventually cleared. The replacement, the 12 flat block, which you can see today, was built in the 1950s to the designs of architect Frederick Thwaites Bush (1887-1985).

Blackheath Vale was a sand pit dug during the 18th century and by the 1760s a substantial hollow. In the deepest part of the Vale one will find

All Saints' Primary School in 1968

the oldest Village primary school – now **All Saints' Blackheath Church of England Primary School**. This may have been founded elsewhere in 1825, but not perhaps built until the 1830s, as a National School of Industry for Girls, teaching domestic economy to about 100 children, the daughters of local working people. In 1867 the school was embraced by the Parish and taken over by the parish council of All Saints' Church, then newly established on the Heath. A plan to build a new school hard by was scotched by strong local opposition under the banner of the Blackheath Improvement Association. The present building dates from about 1877 and an extra classroom block was added in 1939 when the infants, then being taught in the Village school in Tranquil Passage, moved across to Blackheath Vale – almost immediately to be evacuated. To the left of the school is a footpath and steps leading up to the Heath.

Tight close to the school was the **Blackheath Brewery**, established along with a handful of commercial premises including a stonemason's business. The brewery had been well-established by brewer Paul Chits by 1826. Its most famous owner was James Peacock (1812-1882) who produced the standard ales, stouts and porter as well as his extraordinary soapy brew called "Peacock's Swipes" at 1/6d (7½p) a gallon. The brewing stopped in 1875 when its buildings were demolished and the site thrown in to the girls' school (see above) for a playground and, later, an extension classroom. The sides of the Vale most noticeably to the north are protected by a massive concrete retaining wall, which has been known to leak from time to time. The houses on the north-east side of the Vale were built in 1872-74 and named Windsor Villas or Patshull Villas, because Patshull, in Staffordshire, was the seat of the Earls of Dartmouth.

Back now above ground in Duke Humphrey Road there are a few houses built almost at random. **Nos. 5 & 6** Duke Humphrey Road, a pair of houses originally put up in the garden of East Mill House (see below) were originally designated the Retreat; although there is some doubt in the dating of these, 1882 would be a reasonable guess.

Mill on the Heath

From the 1780s until 1887 (more or less) the next plot to the north-east was occupied by East Mill House and the East Mill. While the windmill was demolished after 1832 the substantial house remained and the stump of the mill was evident as late as 1850. In 1885 the Parish purchased East Mill House and demolished it for the **Vicarage** for the incumbent of All Saints' Church. It was designed by local architect Benjamin Tabberer (1831-1910), whose own house stood directly opposite at No 21 Montpelier Row.

Beyond the Vicarage is the group known as **Talbot Place**: two pairs of splendid semi-detached villas of considerable merit built in 1851 on the site of the East Mill. Clearly, these houses were built for the moneyed classes, like those at Vanbrugh Terrace and Aberdeen Terrace, but by the 1930s all had been converted into apartments. **No. 1** (known as Rockingham) was a well-known girls' school, conducted by the Misses Mary and Emily Addison from 1909 to 1919.

History Section 17: Talbot Place to Greenwich Park via the Hub

A fascinating detour to Whitefield's Mount is detailed in the next History Section 18 below, but to follow the main route of the Central Walk strike north from Talbot Place towards Greenwich Park along the gravel-surfaced foot and cycle path; this used to be Duke Humphrey Road.

After a few hundred yards you will meet a circle of flat granite paving stones, which has recently been dubbed the Hub of the Heath. The positions of Lincoln, Church and West Kent Fields and the Old Donkey Pit can be identified from their inscriptions in the outer stone ring. Long Pond Road would have crossed this point from east to west, but is now also reduced to a foot and cycle path. You can see to the east the roundabout on the A2, which encompasses the hillock known as Camomile Bottom. When you have identified all of these features, continue in a northerly direction, cross Shooters Hill Road at the pedestrian traffic lights and you will see the Blackheath Gate to Greenwich Park in front of you. This ends the Central Walk, but you could now start the East Walk or return to Blackheath Village by doing the West Walk in reverse.

The main north-south axis across the Heath is named after Humphrey, Duke of Gloucester (1391-1447) who is remembered for his act of enclosing 74 hectares (183 acres) of Blackheath for his private residence and park. Being the brother of Henry V, it was not difficult for him to obtain Crown consent for his plan, which stretched from the present Greenwich Park wall in the south, down to the line of Park Vista in Greenwich – once all part of the Heath.

The east-west axis was originally just a footpath, which grew into a cart track and, eventually, into Long Pond Road, metalled and drained and much used in recent times by rat-runners and for free and easy parking, particularly by coaches from central London. Vehicles caused erosion

Old Long Pond Road with new Heritage Lamps in February 2012

The official opening of the Hub in June 2012

to the Heath surface and the road widened. After a lengthy campaign to return this and other Heath roads to footpaths, the Blackheath Society finally achieved success in 2000. Long Pond Road stretched across Prince Charles Road, to Riding Field and then across Morden Field – all now returned to the status of foot and cycle paths. The mix of modern lamp standards, many in the wrong positions for the reduced width paths, were replaced in 2012-13 with designs more in keeping with the late 19th century, thanks to a grant from English Heritage.

On the cross roads of the paths still called Duke Humphrey Road and Long Pond Road is the stone **Hub** – a circle of granite created for the Blackheath Society at the suggestion many years before by James Hazlerigg-Kinlay; it was designed by architect Charlie MacKeith and built by Messrs Conway Contractors. The Hub was generously supported by Lewisham Council. It marks the three major events of 2012: HM The Queen's 60th anniversary of her succession to the throne, the XXXth Olympiad of the Modern Era (2012) and the Blackheath Society's 75th birthday, having been founded in January 1937; it is difficult indeed to decide which of these events is the most significant. The Hub was declared "open" on 24 June 2012 by Lewisham MP, Ms Heidi Alexander, and the Mayor of Lewisham Sir Stephen Bullock.

The Heath to the west of Duke Humphrey Road is dominated by **West Kent Field** – which took its name from the cricket club – the West Kent Wanderers – a team made up of artisans and shopkeepers, not usually considered suitable for membership of the Blackheath Cricket Club. The WKW was formed by the landlord of the Hare & Billet in 1859 and named West Kent in 1870, and they tended and used a sizeable cricket table on the north side of Blackheath Vale until 1939. An agreement with the Board of Works was made in 1871 that the cricket table on the field

Cricket on West Kent Field in c.1905

would be held by the Wanderers by right, and that the Club should not be required to join in a "first-come first-served" arrangement nor be treated "on the same level with inferior clubs". After further complaint in 1905, it was agreed the club could tend its own pitch.

This arrangement lasted well, but in 1939 the members were dismayed to see their long cherished table ploughed up for an anti-aircraft detector screen. After the war the West Kent CC moved to the sports field in the south-west corner of Greenwich Park, where they played until 1970, returning to the Heath only when their original ground was restored for their centenary match.

The **Old Donkey Pit** to the north-west has long gone, probably filled and levelled in the 19th century. The tea hut in the far north-west corner, alas, has not. Although it may provide a useful facility for commercial drivers, it has little history, despite its self-proclaimed foundation date. In the late 19th century there was a horse trough on the west side of Goffers Road, close to the junction with the A2 (Shooters Hill Road); and there was a horse drawn "tea hut" on that site in the 1920s. The current enterprise dates from about the late 1950s, although the original post-war hut on the A2 was replaced after an accident in 1971.

Lewisham Council has recently attempted to prevent erosion of the Heath by the parking of vehicles using the tea hut, by installing posts and bunds along Goffers Road. The prevention of parking on the Heath has proved successful, but the re-establishment of grass has proved elusive due to long periods of dry weather and heavy footfall in the area. The Old Donkey Pit field is now used with Lewisham Council's consent by travelling and tented circuses usually for several weeks at a time at the end of the summer or in the spring.

On the north-east side of the hub is Lincoln Field, so named because the Lincoln Regiment bivouacked there during the Great War (1914-1918) before being shipped off to the Front in France. To the furthest east of Lincoln Field is the **roundabout** – established and in operation by 1930 around a small hillock still known as **Camomile Bottom**. The modern traffic management scheme dates from the 1950s. For many years it boasted an attractive garden of small trees, shrubs and bedding plants – but these have been mostly reduced to a grass scrub and a couple of trees. A plan in 2001 to put traffic lights here was frustrated.

New bund near Camomile Bottom in June 2013

The field is also the customary base for the public firework display on the Saturday night closest to November 5th, which has been attended by up to 100,000 people.

November 5th Fireworks on Lincoln Field in 2012

The final quadrant observable to the south-east when standing at the Hub is **Church Field**. The Blackheath Proprietary School played their athletics, rugby-style football and cricket games here from about 1860 until they obtained their own playing field on Manor Way. The tradition however continues today with many organised formal soccer matches taking place at weekends as well as numerous ad hoc groupings. Also,

until about the turn of the last century it was the site for the annual Blackheath Village "Fayre" and then the Blackheath Bike and Kite Festival, which took its place in June for a few years, until hard economic times brought that to an end as well.

It is worth noting that although the names of the various fields used above – West Kent, Lincoln, and Church - have come to be adopted as though of ancient lineage they are all in fact comparatively modern.

When you have crossed over Shooters Hill Road you rejoin the final remaining segment of Duke Humphrey Road and will find the **donkey ride** (see West walk) on your left and **Circus Field** (see East Walk) on your right. At the northern end of the donkey ride there is large metal notice board with a map of the Heath very similar to the one provided with this book.

Donkey Ride, Duke Humphrey Road in c.1980

The stub of Duke Humphrey Road, which used to run from north to south across the Heath, is often dominated during weekdays by the illegal parking of coaches sometimes in rows two deep and occasionally even three deep. The Blackheath Society has campaigned actively for at least fifteen years for this practice to end and for the whole area to be redesigned with an approach to the Greenwich Park World Heritage Site more worthy of its status and also more in keeping with the nature of the Heath, but to no avail. Hopes were raised prior to 2012 that the Olympic Delivery Authority would provide some funding in gratitude for their use of Circus Field as a logistics compound for the Equestrian Events, but this legacy did not materialise.

History Section 18: Detour from Talbot Place to Whitefield's Mount

An interesting short detour from the Central Walk is to turn west at Talbot Place and follow the road until you come to Goffers Road. Cross over here and walk around Whitefield's Pond and Mount in front of you.

You can then rejoin the Central Walk by cutting across the Heath in an easterly direction or return to the Village via Goffers Road. If you do the latter, make a point of looking down at Blackheath Vale, which you can do easily from the narrow footpath and then steps which cross from the Road to the Vale about halfway along.

In 1961, on the scrap of land next to the pair of large semi-detached houses in Talbot Place, the local authority (London County Council) erected **changing rooms** in a typical early sixties architectural style and a car park for the benefit of the sportsmen using the Heath. At the time there were dozens of football pitches and, in summer, not a few cricket tables. Because of a decline in participation in field sports the numbers using the changing rooms seriously declined in the 1990s and, presently (summer 2013), they are closed and demolition is being discussed. There is a map of the Heath on the outer wall, and behind the buildings there is a depot with access from the car park for Glendale, who maintains that part of the Heath which is embraced by the Borough of Lewisham.

The Dartmouth Estate gave consent in 1770 for the building of two windmills on the land to the north of the sand pits, which are now Blackheath Vale. The west side boasted the post mill which stood from 1772 to 1832 on a site now occupied by an attractive 1830s semi-detached house called **Mill House**; just around the corner to the south is the entrance to **Golf House**, its other half. The original name was Heath Hall, but from 1910-1950 it was owned by the Royal Blackheath Golf Club.

When the Golf Club left the Heath in 1923 their old club house was retained, but as a social centre, until the late 1940s. Although sold as a private house it enjoys the name Golf House. The stables and coach house for Heath Hall were converted into a meeting room for the Ladies Blackheath Golf Club, but was subsequently extended and named Sergison Cottage.

The walker will have to exercise care to cross what has been called Goffers Road since 1933, but was formerly known as Windmill Road,

Whitefield's Mount with St Germans Place behind in 1850

obviously because of the nearby windmills. The local authority decision was quite daft, considering that the windmills had long gone but so had the golfers since 1923, except for the social club at Heath House.

On the west side of Goffers Road is the only natural hillock still remaining on the Heath. It is a curiosity in that it is the one place on the Heath that has long boasted a clump of trees indicating a water source deep below the ground. **Whitefield's Mount** is one of the significant points in the topographical history of Blackheath generally, as well as for the Heath. There is circumstantial evidence that it was in place before the 2nd Millennium when it acted as the meeting point for those involved in the administration of a widespread district known as the Hundred of Blackheath.

In some eyes the ground here has a mystical quality, but this may stem from its use for religious meetings in the 18th century.

William Lambarde (1536-1601), Blackheath's first historian, declared that his father could remember the Crown's armourers' forge at the Mount during the Battle of Blackheath Field (1497). John Evelyn noted in his Dairy in April 1687 that he attended a mortar firing exercise at the Mount (later referred to as the Mount for Trying Mortars) "*I saw a trial of those devilish murdering mischief-doing engines called bombes, shot out of a mortar piece on Blackheath. The distance they are cast and the destruction they make and where they fall is prodigious*".

Some decades later the Mount became an open air pulpit, especially for the Methodist cause, with John Wesley (1703-1791) and others preaching to huge crowds (although how anyone could hear what was said is hard to imagine). Wesleyan Methodism was promoted in particular by George Whitefield (1714-1770) and such was his magnetism that his name became attached to the Mount (and the neighbouring Pond) ever since. These sermons are still remembered by ecumenical Easter services to the present day, attracting large congregations in the 1930s – for instance, over 4,000 in 1934.

Whitefield's pond and mount in c.1905

In 1871 the Board of Works erected a fence, and then railings, to protect the Mount from vandals. This was reduced to a paling fence in the middle years of the 1990s and in more recent times protection has been entirely withdrawn. As a result hooliganism and rubbish dumping has increased, and in 2011 a bad fire denuded much of the gorse and scorched the trees. The gorse has regenerated vigorously from its roots, but only one of the trees survived; volunteers planted some replacements in the autumn of 2012, but these failed to thrive through the following dry summer.

The **pond** in front of the Mount, which also bears Whitefield's name, contains water in wet periods, but with a reduced rainfall can completely dry out. It provides an attractive feature on the Heath, particularly when the irises flower in May. As an occasional pond it is relatively rare and therefore much valued for its unusual biodiversity, although its appearance can easily be spoilt by rubbish, which for obvious reasons tends to collect there. The Heath surprisingly has a total of four ponds on it – the others being: the Prince of Wales, the Hare and Billet, and the Folly – and they each have their own individual character and fans. Two others, Real pond and Circus Pit pond - have long gone.

Central Walk Summary

Road	Building/Feature	Map No.	His. Sec.
Royal Parade	Start of Walk		15
	All Saints' Church	59	
	Drinking Fountain	64	
	Tranquil Hall (well) in Village	65	
Footpath across Heath	Washerwomen's Bottom	61	15
Duke Humphrey Road (south section)	Goffers House (Talbot Houses)	129	16
Blackheath Vale	All Saints Primary School (Blackheath Brewery)	56	16
Duke Humphrey Road (south section)	Nos 5, 6 (the Retreat)		16
	The Vicarage (East Mill House)	55	
Talbot Place	No. 1 (Girls' School)		16
Footpath across Heath (Old Duke Humphrey Road)	The Hub on the Heath		17
	Old Long Pond Road		
	West Kent Field (cricket)		
	Old Donkey Pit (circuses)		
	Lincoln Field (fireworks)		
	Church Field (Village Fayre)		
Shooters Hill Road	Cross A2 at lights		
Duke Humphrey Road (north section)	Donkey ride, Circus Field	47	17
	Blackheath Gates to Park	45	
	Finish of Central Walk		
Talbot Place (a detour)	Changing rooms (Lewisham)	52	18
	Mill and Golf House	51,53	
Goffers Road	Whitefield's Mount (mortars)	37	18
	Whitefield's Pond (occasional)	38	

Acknowledgements

The authors are most grateful for the assistance given in a variety of measures, by many people and organisations, to the content of this walker's guide to the history and topography of Blackheath.

Blackheath Society archives and illustrations collection
The Blackheath Preservation Trust Ltd
Blackheath Joint Working Party
The British Library
The London Library
Times Digital
City of London History Library, Guildhall
Heritage Centre, Royal Borough of Greenwich
Local History Library, Lewisham Council

- -

Allan Griffin (Archive Project Leader)
Ruth Le Guen (design)
David Notton (for matters ecological)
Wendy Shelton
Jo Swadkin (Timeline)
Howard Shields
Frank Smith
Greycot Press

Trevor Diggens
Helen Doris
Ralph Hyde
Jean Le Guen
Ann Longrigg
Manzur Maula
Mary Mills
Dr Ian Roy

Val Salmond
Sue Shields
Philip Smith
Catherine Walton
Julian Watson
Hilary Weedon
Liz Wright

Principal sources

Most of the historical detail in both the *Walk* and the *Timeline* comes from the 2nd edition of Neil Rhind's *Heath* (Bookshop, London, 2002). Not currently [2013] in print but available in local libraries and antiquarian bookshops

Metropolitan Board of Works minutes 1860-1889

London County Council (later Greater London Council) minutes 1889-1970

Rate books and vestry minutes of the parishes of Greenwich, Lewisham, Charlton and the Liberty of Kidbrooke

Blackheath Society: Annual Reports 1938-2012, Newsletters, Council (Committee) minutes; and other publications

Transactions of the Greenwich & Lewisham Antiquarian Society (later the Greenwich Historical Society)

Blackheath Local Guide &District Advertiser (and subsequent titles) 1889-1957; 1959-2000

The (Kentish) M*ercury* (and all previous and subsequent titles) 1833-2012

The Times: 1785-2010

Illustrations

All the illustrations have been taken from the Society's images collection. Some copyrights and ownerships are held by others and these are acknowledged wherever possible in the captions. If anything has been omitted or erroneously captioned we apologise and will endeavour to correct mistakes on the next edition.

Overleaf: *HM Queen Victoria and HRH Prince Albert review the massed troops on a rather fanciful Blackheath in 1841.* Perhaps the artist confused it with a similar event at Richmond. By kind permission of the Royal Borough of Greenwich Heritage Centre.

Die Königl. Grossbrittanische Armée Revüe. 1ᵉʳ ABTH. ⟨crest⟩ Tableau General de l'Armée R. Britanique. (1ᵉʳ SECT.)

Dedié à Son Altesse Royal Mons. Albrecht Duc de Saxe Cobourg Gotha &c &c.

50

A Blackheath Timeline

By Neil Rhind
assisted by Jo Swadkin and Roger Marshall

10,000 BC – Forest fires denuded large areas of Wealden Kent of its forests (the *Anderida*). Some areas, like Blackheath and Dartford Heath were so scorched that nothing grew for centuries except gorse and heather. At least, in south-east London, the fires cleared a wide open belt down to the River Thames which would have encouraged settlement.

1st to the 4th centuries – Roman occupation. Artefacts found at Dartmouth Row and the remains of a temple and other archaeological finds across the south section of Greenwich Park

Roman road cuts across the north east corner of Greenwich Park and Westcombe Park to join the line of what is now the Old Dover Road and onwards as Shooters Hill.

The Heath, an open treeless plain, originally about 304 hectares (750 acres) stretched roughly from Deptford on the west, to Kidbrooke on the east and Lee on the south to the River Thames in the north

----

5th & 6th centuries - Saxon barrows on the Heath and in what became Greenwich Park. Chalk digging creates caverns under the Point

848 – Charter granting local lands attributed to Elstrudis, daughter of Alfred (the Great)

1011-1014 – Danish invasions – occupation of Greenwich

1012 – Danes kill Alfege, Archbishop of Canterbury, allegedly on what became the site for Greenwich Parish church

1086 - Domesday Book makes first reference to a centre of local social administration: the "Hundred of Greneviz". Elders meet at the Mount on the Heath - now called Whitefield's Mount.

1166 – Documents relating to the Hundred of Blackheath in the Pipe rolls refer to *Blachehedfeld*

1170 – Pilgrims anxious to worship at the shrine of Thomas Becket, at Canterbury, rest on the Heath during their journey

1227 – Groom to the Earl of Gloucester murdered at the Stone Cross on *Blakehatfeuld*

1255 – "*Malefactors unknown met Hamo of Chetwode and Roger le Jeune at Blakehethe and attack them and they wound the said Hamo in the arm and he died and whence they are is unknown.*"

1274 – The King is the Lord of the Hundred of Blackheath in the Last of Sutton

1293 – First reference to Blackheath - as a residential place – when John, a baker of *Blakehetefelde*, was accused of robbery but found not guilty by a local jury

1301 – Abbey of Ghent rents some land next to the Heath: "*La Blakehethe*"

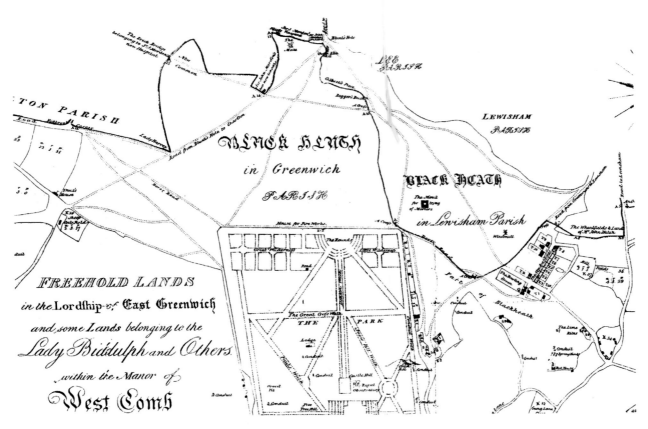

Travers survey 1695-96

1316 – The Sovereign is the Lord of the Hundred of Blackheath

July 1323 – Marie de St Pol met on Blackheath by Edward II's knights after her marriage to Aymer De Valence, Earl of Pembroke.

1349-1350 – Ravages of the so-called "Black Death". Huge numbers died in the locality but Blackheath is not named because of this, nor was it a burial ground

1373 – Death of John Northwode, mercer of London, on *Blake Hethe*, at a wrestling match

1381 – Peasants' Revolt against the imposition of a three groats (5p) a head Poll Tax, led by Wat Tyler and Jack Straw. Uprising failed and many of the leaders killed, including Wat Tyler; Jack Straw and others were executed.

1387 – Chaucer's *Canterbury Tales* mentions Blackheath

1390 – Richard II welcomed home on Blackheath after his marriage to the daughter of Chares IV, King of France

December 1400 – Manuel Palaeologus, Emperor of Byzantium, seeking help in his war against the Turks, met on Blackheath by Henry IV

1414 – Dissolution of the alien priories by Henry V. Lewisham and Greenwich granted to the Carthusian Abbey of Shene. All monasteries finally dissolved by Henry VIII in 1539-40

November 1415 – Henry V welcomed home by citizens and civic dignitaries after his victory at Agincourt. Henry ignored the *"vaine pompe and shewes as in triumphant sort devised for his welcoming home ..."*

May 1416 – Sigismund, Emperor of Germany, met the king on Blackheath to negotiate a peace between England and France

February 1431 – Henry VI (1427-1471) met on Blackheath by London's civic dignitaries after his coronation in Paris

December 8 1432 – Humphrey, Duke of Gloucester (d1447), brother of Henry V, granted consent to enclose 74 hectares (183 acres) of Blackheath for a private park (now Greenwich Park). The first major encroachment of Blackheath. Remained the Crown's private property after Humphrey's untimely death.

May 1445 – Margaret of Anjou (d1482) welcomed by Humphrey, Duke of Gloucester, on Blackheath before her marriage to Henry VI and their Coronation on 30 May 1445

1450 – The Heath was the camping ground for Jack Cade and his followers when presenting the *Blackheath Petition* to "... punish evil ministers and procure a redress of grievance." The rebels: *"rebellious hinds, the filth and scum of Kent"* according to Sir Humphrey Stafford [quoted in Shakespeare's *Henry VI*, (Part 2, Act IV, Scene II)].

1452 – Armed revolt by Duke of York, who had openly claimed the crown. Henry VI positioned his army on Blackheath and tricked York into surrender.

May 1471 - Thomas Fauconberg (or Falconbridge) a supporter of the king, retreats to Blackheath after Henry defeated at Tewsksbury by Edward IV.

1474 – Edward IV welcomed home from France by the Lord Mayor of London and citizens in their best clothes. Edward, backed by an army of 30,000, had signed a treaty with Louis XI of France.

Wricklemarsh House

June 1497 – Battle of Blackheath Field. A rebellion by Cornishmen, to protest at having to pay taxes to fund the King's Scottish wars. With their leaders Thomas Flammock and Michael Joseph – 6,000 camped on the Heath and fought the army of Henry VII. Many were killed – from as few as 300 and up to 2,000, reports vary wildly - and legend claims they were buried on the Heath. The leaders were executed. In June 1997 the London Cornish Association and the Cornish Gorsedd arranged for a memorial plaque to be fixed to the south face of Greenwich Park wall, close to the southern gate, to mark the 500th anniversary of the Battle.

May 1512 – The eccentric Guyot of Guy accompanied by 500 Almaines (German mercenaries) offers his troop to the King's benefit. He was knighted, awarded an annual pension and sent to Southampton where he could do no harm.

1518 – Lord Ronevet, Admiral of France and Bishop of Paris, with a retinue of 1,200 was met on the Heath by the Lord High Admiral of England and a more modest band of 500 retainers

July 1518 – Cardinal Lorenzo Campeggio (1472-1539) arrived in England, is met on Blackheath and installed as Ambassador from the Vatican. He changed into his cardinal's robes at Blackheath and was accompanied to London by 2,000 horsemen.

1540 – Henry VIII stages a Second Field of the Cloth of Gold to mark his first meeting with Anne of Cleves. The east side of the Heath pitched with tents, gold cloth, pavilions and the trappings of a Royal picnic. A passage was cut through the gorse and Henry led Anne to Greenwich with great and expensive ceremony, where he married her. A union which did not last.

1550s – Edward VI with his court frequently rode on Blackheath.

1570 – William Lambarde (1536-1601), Blackheath's first historian, claimed in his *Perambulations of Kent* that the smith's forge for the armourers at the Battle of Blackheath Field (1497) was the hillock we call Whitefield's Mount.

April 1585 – Elizabeth I was offered a demonstration of affection and loyalty by the City Militia. Five thousand of them camped on the Heath for eight days.

1608 – James I (VI of Scotland) credited with the introduction of golf into England and the establishment of a golfing club or society at Blackheath. Pure legend.

1619-1624 – Greenwich Park fence replaced with 12ft brick wall

With the departure of the Royal Court from Greenwich after 1625 there was an immediate decline in its use as a Royal parade ground until the mid 18th century

1629 – First recorded appearance of the Green Man public house at the top of Blackheath Hill. Three times rebuilt and the last version demolished 1970.

1635 – Clothing of plague victims burned on the Heath

1642 – Civil War: The meeting of the Kentish Men on the Heath, and the pamphlet – *News from Blackheath.*

November 1642 - Charles I grants a pardon to all those "... *who had been induced to exercise the Militia on Blackheath under cover of a pretended ordinance.*"

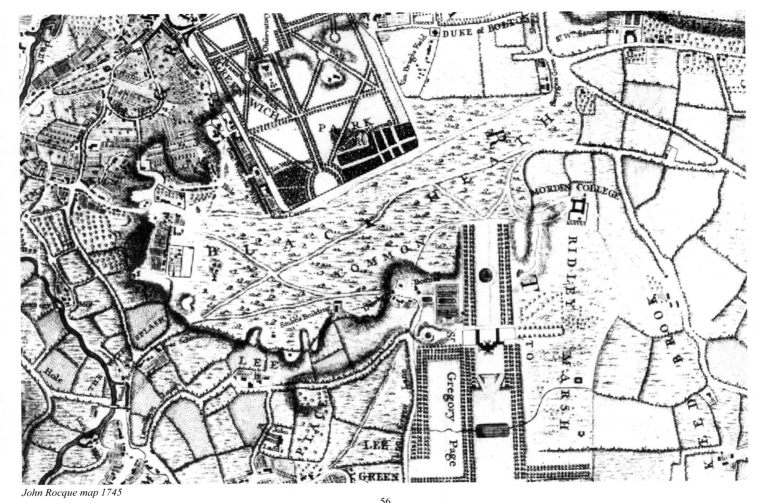

John Rocque map 1745

1645 - Local Blackheath landowner Col Thomas Blount (1605-1678) exercised two regiments of foot in a sham fight as though between Cavaliers and Roundheads. *"The people were as much pleased as if they had gone a-maying"*

1648 – *The Petition of Kent*: Royalist forces confronted by General Thomas Fairfax (1612-1671), accompanied by 7,000 troops. The Royalists retreated to Rochester and were routed eventually at Maidstone

1656 – John Evelyn (1620-1706) witnesses the "plows and a coach waywiser" tested on Blackheath by Thomas Blount

1659 – General Fairfax encamps with two companies of militia "... for preservation of the citizens in the present danger .."

1660 – Big turn out on Blackheath to welcome Charles II on the Restoration of the Monarchy, the first of many ceremonies to lead to his coronation on 23 April 1661.

1665 – Samuel Pepys (1633-1703) watches demonstrations of a wicker chariot. *"After dinner comes Collonel Blount in his new Charriott made with Springs as that was of wicker wherein since we rode at his house. ... so for curiosity I went in to try it and up the hill to the Heath and over the cart ruts went to try it, and found it pretty well but not so easy at he pretends".*

1673 – John Evelyn recorded: *"We went after dinner to see the formal and formidable camp on Blackheath raised to invade Holland, or, as others suspected, for another design".* He noted the encampment of about 4,000 soldiers which inspired the verse-pamphlet: *News from the Camp on Blackheath* or *the Noble Soldier's Resolution.*

1680s – Encroachment of a windmill and watchtower on the Heath near Dartmouth Terrace

May 1683 – Licence granted for a three day fair (twice a year, in May and October) on the edge of the Heath close to Dartmouth Row (on the "Fairfield"). Initially for the sale of bullocks and horses – curtailed to one day in 1772. Interest dwindled by 1860. Abolished in 1872.

1687 – John Evelyn's *Diary* records that he saw on the Mount *"A trial of those devilish murdering mischief-doing engines called bombes, shot out of a mortar piece on Blackheath. The distance that they are cast and the destruction where they fall is prodigious"*

1689 – Houses being erected on the edge of the Heath at Dartmouth Row (an encroachment) and West Grove

July and August 1690 – Evelyn records: *"Major Andrew Birch now quartered with the Regiment (newly come out of Flanders) dined with me; and this afternoon began to incamp upon Blackheath .... Limrick (sic) not yet reduced. Our Camp at Blackheath marching to Portsmouth"*

1695-1696 – *Survey of His Majesty's Lordship or Manor of East Greenwich* by Samuel Travers, confirms public use of the Heath (manorial waste) lawful but not any abuse of it – such as illegal gravel digging, rubbish dumping, encroachments for building, etc

1699-1700 – Development along Greenwich Park Wall: Admiral Hosier's (later Rangers) House, houses for the Earls of Derby, and others

1702 – The Chocolate House, a place of "fashionable assembly" on what is now West Grove, opened by Thomas Tozier (d1733), the King's Chocolate maker. Headquarters for the Blackheath golfers and other sporting and social clubs. Converted to educational use in 1789. Finally demolished 1886.

1709 – Several thousand Palatine refugees camp in tents on Blackheath because the City feared epidemics.

Woodlands House, Myceane Road

1719-1721 – Sir John Vanbrugh (1664-1726) designs a mock medieval village on the north side of the Heath. Vanbrugh Castle (his own home) survives

1720-1820 – Large number of highway robberies and street crimes on Blackheath reported in the local and national press. From 1800 decline in highway robbery and a big increase in burglary

1723 – Building of Wricklemarsh House, for Sir Gregory Page (1689-1775) just off south-east edge of the Heath

1728 – George II journeys to Blackheath to review Kirk's and Harrison's regiments, afterwards dining with Gregory Page at Wricklemarsh

1730 – Encroachment for Hare & Billet public house and cottages and, eventually, for Grotes Place

1742 – Army camps on the Heath, reviewed by George II before they marched off to Gravesend to embark for Flanders. Local resident Lt-General Sir Philip Honywood (1678-1752) takes charge until the arrival of the King and his Field Marshal John Dalrymple (1673-1747), 2nd Earl of Stair

1745 – Jacobite invasion scare sees the raising of local battalions; Gregory Page raises one of 500 men probably more to protect his fine house and family rather than for the safety of the nation.

1750s – Eastnor House and Lloyds Place triangle taken from the Heath

1753 – Because of the high level of criminality the Blackheath Association to Prevent Crime – Joseph Lock, High Constable - is established. Failed in its purpose.

1756 – Hermitage encroachment near Eliot Pits

1762 – The Pagoda, Eliot Vale, summer house for Montague House which stood on the south-west corner of Greenwich Park, built on south side of the Heath

1766 - Expatriate Scotsmen – mostly Edinburgh merchants and members of the Honourable Company of Edinburgh Golfers – establish a branch of their golfing society on Blackheath. It survives today as the Royal Blackheath Golf Club, the oldest such outside Scotland

1768-1770 – Major infrastructure plans for Blackheath roads and planting; sheep farming to be encouraged.

June 1770 – George III and HRH the Duke of Cumberland review the 3rd Regiment of Foot Guards.

1771– A grand straight road from London Bridge via Greenwich to Woolwich is planned. Brick wall to Greenwich Park to be pulled down and iron rails (with a sunken fence towards the Heath) to be placed in its stead

1772 – The King reviewed the 3rd and 4th battalions of the Royal Regiment of Artillery. *"Greatly incommoded by the weather and obstructed by a prodigious concourse of people."*

1775 – Two windmills erected on edge of sandpit (Blackheath Vale)

1778 – The Blackheath Rangers to be formed – a body of 1,000 men. Nothing happened.

1780 – Troops camp on Blackheath during the Gordon Riots

1780 – Chalk caverns "discovered" under The Point

1781 – The Orchard encroachment for large private house and garden

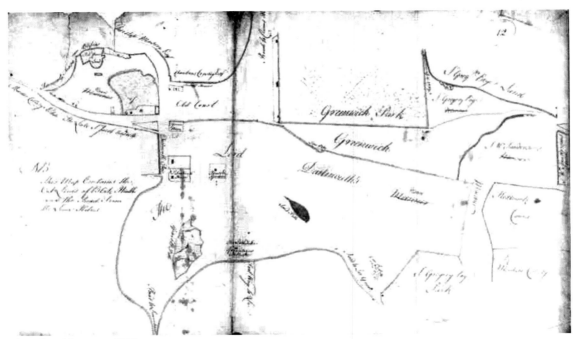

Lewisham Manor map 1755

August 1786 - *"A trial was made on Blackheath of a machine to sail by land which went at a great rate till the mast broke, and by that accident the rudder and some other parts received material injury."*

1788 – George III visits the Heath three times that year, twice in May, once to review General Pitt's Regiment of Dragoons. The King left Buckingham House at 8.15am and was back home by 11.30am.

1789 – Meetings of the Toxopholite Society

1790 – The British Amazons (an "elegant and beauteous" toxopholite society for women) meet on the Heath

1790-1810 – Shops and houses extending the Village built on Heath land

1791 - Foundations for the Paragon development first laid – crescent not fully complete until 1805

1792 – Formation of a Blackheath Association for the prevention of robbery. Failed to do so

1793 - Big fire when gipsies, encamped at Eliot Vale, set fire to the gorse

1796 – The beginning of Eliot Place and Eliot Vale

1798 – Blackheath Volunteer Cavalry & Loyal Greenwich Volunteers formed – a troop of 50 men under the Command of Capt Maryon Wilson. Disbanded 1809

11 May 1798 – Duel between William Ross and Lt. David Reid of the Bengal Army. Ross killed, supposedly the last known fatality from a duel in Britain.

1799 – HRH Princess Caroline of Brunswick (1768-1821), estranged wife of the Heir apparent – Prince George - moved to Blackheath and takes on Montague House, on the south-west corner of Greenwich Park, and the Pagoda garden pavilion on the other side of the Heath.

1801 – John Julius Angerstein (1735-1823), resident at Woodlands, Westcombe Park, illegally enclosed 11 hectares (26.5 acres) of Blackheath on the north side of Shooters Hill Road. Deal made with the Parish but land not developed until 1839.

May 1804 – Colours presented to Blackheath Cavalry by Lord Mayor of London at massive display of local volunteer regiments from all over London, including the River Fencibles. The display occupied a space of three square miles. The reports suggested that 16,000 volunteers were present.

September 1806 - Duel between Baron Hompesch, who raised a regiment during the Irish rebellion of 1798, and a Mr Richardson. Richardson wounded in the hip.

1812 - Big fire when an enthusiastic local population set fire to the gorse to celebrate the birthday of HRH the Princess of Wales then living at Montague House, on the corner of Greenwich Park

1812 – Meeting to urge improvement of the "local police force". Nothing happened

1813 – HRH Caroline Princess of Wales left Montague House. The building demolished in 1815, some said out of the spite of her husband, the Prince Regent (later George IV)

September 1815 – George Wilson the "Blackheath Pedestrian" attempted to walk a 1,000 miles in 1,000 hours around Blackheath but failed this time because he was stopped walking on the Sabbath. Others copied his feat, including Josiah Eaton who aimed to cover 1,100 miles in 1,100 hours. Pedestrianism remained popular until the 1860s.

Review of the ARCHERS on Blackheath.

1820 – Association for Punishing and Preventing Offences within the District of Blackheath established. No greater success than previous schemes.

1825 – Local cricket first recorded using pitches on the Heath: Dartmouth CC and Paragon CC most famous

1826 – Blackheath Brewery established in Blackheath Vale. Famous for its "Peacock's Swipes". Closed 1875.

1827 – "Real" [Royal] pond on the Dover Road (A2) filled up and consolidated.

1830s – Donkey and pony rides started near the Blackheath Gate entrance to the Park

January 1831 – Foundation of the Blackheath Proprietary School. Closed 1907. The school played its games (athletics, cricket, hockey and, later, a rugby style football) on the Heath from the mid 1850s and for many years. Old boys responsible for the foundation of the Blackheath Football Club in 1862.

February 1834 – John Gee ran a mile in 4min 53sec

May 1834 – Three mile trotting races on Heath – the three miles between stones on Shooters Hill and the Green Man, Blackheath Hill

July 1835 – Gipsies a major nuisance, especially fortune tellers

1836 – Windmills on the edge of Blackheath Vale taken down

September 1836 – Pedestrians completed 50 miles in 9hrs 20mins

November 1840 – Thousands turned out to watch popular field games

1842 -1843– Temperance meetings allegedly attracted 50,000

October 1842 – Running matches on Heath from Green Man to top of Shooters Hill – watched by a crowd estimated at 5,000.

December 1842 – Eight thousand gathered to watch a mile race (5min 10 sec) and other sports in pouring rain. "*No police around to mar the sport".*

1844 & 1848 – Chartist rallies

1844-1845 – Reservoir originally planned for Blackheath, opposite Rangers House, sited in Greenwich Park after public outcry

1846 – Shinty played on Blackheath

July 1849 – Blackheath Railway Station opened for passenger traffic

1849-1850 – *David Copperfield*, by Charles Dickens (1812-1870). Creakle's Academy supposedly based on the Chocolate House Academy, once in West Grove

December 1850– Anti-papist rallies – effigies of the Pope and cardinals burned, and for many years thereafter

1852 – Blackheath Volunteer Rifle Corps established, eventually part of the West Kent Militia

1853 – *Bal masque* in the Cavern under Point Hill ended in pitch dark and chaos and cavern closed permanently thereafter

1853 – Big anti-catholic demonstrations. Ritual burning of effigies of the Pope and Cardinals

1855 – Blackheath Gate to Greenwich Park erected and entrance widened. Smaller entrance for cyclists added 1900-1901. Whole restructured and shape altered 2012

October 1855 – Fireworks and bonfires to mark the fall of Sebastopol (Crimean campaign) – a year after the event. 30,000 gathered on the Heath for the evening's spectacular entertainment.

The Heath, covered in rough gorse and heather - note the bridge over one of the old gravel pits.
Engraved by W Noble, 1805

1856 – Formation of the Blackheath Improvement Association. Volunteers divide Heath into four segments to clear up litter, remove graffiti, remove dead dogs from ponds and undertake a little tree surgery and planting. Eventually wound up in the late 1860s when it changed its name to the Blackheath Preservation Society to lobby for the takeover of the Heath by the Board of Works

November 1858 – All Saints' Church opened for worship on All Saints' Day

1859 – 3rd Kent Rifle Volunteers formed

1859 – Survey of the flora and fauna of Blackheath by the Greenwich Natural History Society

March 1860 – Artillery Volunteers (5th Battalion 1st Brigade Kent Artillery)   established headquarters in disused chapel on Dartmouth Hill. Flagstaff and gun battery sited on Heath

1861 – Drill Shed erected for 25th West Kent (Blackheath) Volunteer Rifle Corps at the west end of Vanbrugh Park

1861 – Formation of the Blackheath Hockey Club, the oldest surviving hockey club in the world. Dormant during Great War but revived in 1925. Now plays at its own ground at Catford.

March 1861 – Grumbles that gentry exercise their horses on the Greenwich Lads' cricket ground

1861 – Kidbrooke Volunteer Rifle Corps hold manoeuvres on the Heath

Autumn 1862 – Blackheath Football Club played first match, with Rugby School rules (roughly). By the 1870s crowds forced play off the Heath, eventually to the Club's own ground - Rectory Field - on Charlton Road.

October 1862 – Pro-Garibaldi meeting

February 1864 – Naked men seen running on Heath – *"hideous nightmare ... abominable occurrences"*, say the residents

January 1865 – Blackheath Improvement Association said that ponies and horses were an increasing nuisance on Heath. Petition to Secretary of State started to seek Parliamentary protection for the Heath.

March 1865 – Major digging for gravel in Circus Pit. Massive outcry. Banned by June 1868.

1867 – Blackheath Preservation Society – a lobbying group – forced Parliament to pass the Metropolitan Commons protective legislation

1868 – Anti-Heath protection movement – *"won't end contemporary destruction."*

1868 – Prime Minister William Ewart Gladstone (1809-1898) spoke at the hustings on Blackheath

1869 – Metropolitan Commons Acts designed to take into public care various areas of London's manorial waste and neglected commons

1869 – Peckham Hare & Hounds (founded 1857) established as Blackheath Harriers, an athletics club (now Blackheath & Bromley Harriers) at its new headquarters, the Green Man Public House, east end of Blackheath Hill

March 1869 – Plagues of daddy-long-legs (crane fly, sp *tipula*)

May 1869 - Last gravel extraction (near Vanbrugh Park) before the introduction of bye-laws designed to discourage digging and rubbish dumping

Marrs Ravine and the Hare & Billet pub (right), looking towards Blackheath Village. c1900

1870 – West Kent Wanderers Cricket Club founded by landlord of the Hare & Billet public house. The No 1 Pitch on Blackheath restored for its centenary game in 1970.

June 1870 – Protest meeting against Heath protection – "... *people deprived of their rights of open assembly ...*"

July 1870 – Ha-ha at the Paragon judged not part of the Heath protection scheme

1871 – Supplemental Commons Act confirms Blackheath (manorial waste) has passed into public care with responsibility handed to the Metropolitan Board of Works to maintain the Heath as a place of amenity and recreation for the public in perpetuity.

April 1871 – Horse trough and drinking fountain installed on Dover Road at top of Hyde Vale

December 1871 – Board of Works published first Rules and Regulations for Blackheath

1872 – Riding Ring ("rotten row") established on field between Prince Charles Road and Prince of Wales Road. Not renewed after 1918. Last vestiges lost during levelling works in 1926

1872-1873 - Prince of Wales pond concrete-lined and edged for a boating pond. Inevitable grumbles and protests

February 1872 – Blackheath cattle fairs abolished

March 1872 – Letter in local press claimed Blackheath is "doomed". *..all rights of common extinguished"*

1872-1873 – Gas lamps placed at cross roads. Not converted to electricity until the 1940s.

1873 – Landlord of Princess of Wales public house erected pub sign on the Heath. Initially declared illegal but proved to enjoy prescriptive rights, having been in place for over 40 years.

1874 – Large meeting to support locked-out agricultural labourers. Joseph Arch (1826-1919) speaks.

1876 – Gladstone addressed crowds on the Heath in his campaign against the Turkish atrocities against the Bulgarians

May 1877 – Board of Works decided the Point is dangerous. Protective measures (railings) to be installed

1878 – Major subsidence of 20 feet of a large area near the Riding Field. Similar in 1880 near Eliot Place. Experts judged them to be the collapse of pebbles in dry weather. No pits smelled of sulphur as claimed. Further collapses 1881

1878 – Chocolate Pond, on the north-west side of the Heath and once the largest of the Heath ponds, filled in and consolidated, the horse trough at the top of Hyde Vale having taken over its function.

November 1880 – Major rally of cyclists and tricyclists based on the Green Man

1882 – Metropolitan Lodge (Heath Keeper's House) built on the Heath triangle between Charlton Way and Shooters Hill Road, for Heath Superintendent, Henry Smith. Last resident Heath Keeper, Mr Roy Fox, retired 1991. Restoration completed by March 2002. House reoccupied 2003.

1888 – Folly Pond (sometimes the Boating Pond) created in old gravel pit outside Blackheath Gate on Greenwich Park Wall to help the unemployed

Montpelier Row, Blackheath

1888 – Combined volunteer battalions (the "West Kents") took over Holly Hedge House, onetime residence of the vicars of Lewisham. Freehold obtained in 1906

September 1889 – 500 striking dock workers rallied on Heath with drums, fifes and banners, to collect funds

March 1890 – London County Council decide to lay down 18 fixed cricket pitches for men and a further 18 for boys

January 1891 – LCC lay down a Quoits ground close to All Saints' Church. First come – first served.

1893 – Opportunity to return the Orchard Estate to the Heath rejected by the owners and the land developed for middle class villas (The Orchard and Orchard Drive). Orchard House demolished 1965

1893 – Beer tents at the funfairs abolished

1893 – Last licences issued to washerwomen to dry clothes on the Heath in pit near All Saints' Church (Washerwomen's Bottom)

1896 – Public conveniences installed at back of Heath Keeper's House on Shooters Hill Road

June 1896 – Big fire in Vanbrugh Pits

1897 – Huge bonfire to mark Queen Victoria's Diamond Jubilee

1897 – Memorial drinking fountain erected by Village tradesmen and placed on the Heath, at the junction of Tranquil Vale and Royal Parade, to mark the Diamond Jubilee. Cost was £224 but a shortfall in funding was met by a local authority contribution of £20

July 1897 – Band concerts moved from near All Saints' Church to The Point

May 1899 – First suicide in Folly Pond (Elizabeth Scraggs)

May 1900 – Massive bonfire to mark the end of the Siege of Mafeking

1900-1910 – Huge crowds at Bank Holidays caused considerable nuisance over the decade despite police presence.

October 1900 – Gentlemen's underground lavatory installed opposite Montpelier Row. "... an outrage on good taste ... a piece of Council fussiness and waste ..." Removed in the 1960s

1901 – Edith Nesbit (1858-1924) stories (*Wouldbegoods, Treasure Seekers, etc*) set on Blackheath

August 1902 – Mosquito problem on Blackheath ponds. LCC used petroleum to curb menace – "*won't harm fish*"

1903 – Blackheath and Greenwich Bowling Club green laid down behind Rangers House but later moved to a site next to the tennis court, which had been established in 1923. Since moved to the south of Rangers House

1905 – Proposal to install a light railway or tram lines across the Heath frustrated by strong public opinion.

1907 – Major sewer works across Heath. Ventilation shafts unacceptable say locals

1908 – Marr's Ravine filled up with excavation spoil from the laying down of a major new sewer

1908 – South East Model Yacht Club formed, to be based on Prince of Wales pond. Exclusive use denied by LCC

September 1911 – Blackheath Model Aero Club formed

The Paragon (restored after war damage) and some of Blackheath's prefabs, in 1958

July 1913 – Women's Suffrage meeting. Smaller crowd than expected. No trouble.

July 1914 – Public dancing on the Heath, as well as at Clapham and Hampstead Heath, encouraged by the LCC

September 1914 – Outbreak of Great War (1914-1918). Holly Hedge House opened as a recruitment centre. Troops bivouacked on the Heath throughout hostilities.

September 1914 – Patriotic rally – 40,000 at Whitefield's Mount. Major recruiting opportunity

November 1917 – Local groups demanded air raid shelters to be built on the Heath between All Saints' Church and Duke Humphrey Road

August 1922 – Paddle and row boats for children launched on Folly Pond

November 11 1922 – Dedication of a 1914-1918 War Memorial to the fallen of Greenwich, on the south-east corner of Greenwich Park Wall at the junction of Maze Hill and Charlton Way.

1923 – Royal Blackheath Golf Club left Blackheath, after nearly 200 years, for Eltham. Merger of interests with the Eltham Golf Club.

May 1925 – Arterial road planned to cut off south-east corner of the Heath, in front of The Paragon and Morden College. Huge public protests, scheme abandoned.

1926 - Camomile Bottom (roundabout on A2) to be established. Completed in August 1930.

May-June 1926 – Riding Ring formally abolished

July 1927 - Large advertising hoardings for the Empire Marketing Board removed from Heath after public outcry

1928 – Proposal for a swimming pool near the Eliot Pits frustrated by public opinion

1930s – Ecumenical Good Friday services at Whitefield's Mount. In 1934 the Rev Brian Hession preached to a congregation of over 4,000.

August 1931 – Fountain and shelter to the memory of Greenwich Alderman Andrew Gibb (1853-1908) paid for by his widow's estate. Designed by architect Ernest George Theakston (1878-1943). Restored in November 2003.

1933 – Some Heath roads renamed but much controversy caused as generally judged to be unnecessary: part of Talbot Place became Duke Humphrey Road; Windmill Road became Goffers Road; Woolwich Road became Prince of Wales Road; the Orchard (section towards Crooms Hill) became Whitefield Road; the north end of Lewisham Hill assigned the name Wat Tyler Road although only on a single vote majority by the local authority ruling party.

1934 – Subsidence under east end of Blackheath Hill close to the Point

18 January 1937 – Blackheath Society established

1938 – Historic houses at south (Heath) end of Crooms Hill demolished despite protest.

March 1939 – German plane suffered forced landing next to Talbot Houses, now Duke Humphrey Road. The pilot thought he had landed at Croydon aerodrome

April 1939 – Designs issued for car park and shelters near All Saints' Church. Auxiliary Fire Service practice hose drill using the Prince of Wales pond

Big storm 1987

September 1939 – Outbreak of World War. Trenches and anti-aircraft landing mounds built on Heath.

November 1939 – Caverns under the Point opened and inspected for suitability as air raid shelters. Judged wanting and reclosed.

1940 - Ack-ack gun placements, rocket and searchlight batteries, barrage balloon sites established on Heath and in Greenwich Park

1940-1945 – Nissen huts built on Heath to house military personnel

September 1942 – "Battle of Blackheath" – All Saints' Church "bombed"; Paragon Place "in flames"

November 1946 – US soldiers played baseball on Circus Field

1945-1948 – Bomb rubble was used to fill up old gravel pits at Circus Field, Vanbrugh Terrace, and Washerwomen's Bottom, next to All Saints' Church

September 1946 –Last recruitment column left Blackheath with a military tattoo

1946-1956 – Prefabricated houses built on Heath at St Germans Place and Mounts Pond Road

1946 – Most of Holly Hedge House demolished after bomb damage

1948 – Squatters still occupying abandoned Nissen huts. Heath restoration slows down.

1950 – Life Guards camped on Heath in case of food shortages arising from stevedores strike at the London Docks

December 1951 – Volunteers' Drill Shed on Vanbrugh Park burned down

1959 – Prefabs removed from St Germans Place

1961 – Dressing room facilities for sportsmen built at Talbot Place at a cost of £47,000

1965 – Last prefabs removed from Mounts Pond Road

1965 – First of the Blackheath "May Fayres" was held initially under the auspices of the Blackheath & Charlton Chamber of Trade

1967 – Civic Amenities Act

April 1968 – Large areas of the Blackheath residential suburb including the Heath designated a Conservation Area by London Borough of Greenwich. Similar designation for that part of Blackheath within the London Borough of Lewisham.

1969 – Greater London Development Plan: a London-wide scheme to cut a major motorway through inner London, *inter alia* through Blackheath Village, resisted by the people throughout the Capital.

1970 – Inquiry into proposed road schemes. Alternative version for Blackheath suggested by Professor Colin Buchanan in 1970 proposes a tunnel under the Heath.

1971 - Motorway plan abandoned. No progress on tunnel

1971 – Post-war tea hut destroyed in road traffic incident. Immediately replaced.

1971 – Centenary of the Heath being taken into public care. *Blackheath Centenary 1871-1971* booklet, by Neil Rhind, published by the Greater London Council (GLC)

Litterpickers

1981 - Plan to mark the 600th anniversary of the Peasants' Revolt which involved letting off sections of the Heath to commercial salesmen proved illegal and application withdrawn.

29 March 1981 – 1st London Marathon started on Blackheath and at the Blackheath Gate to Greenwich Park. It has remained an established feature of each year since.

1983 – Long hot summer damaged Heath. Much erosion, and Folly Pond and Whitefield's Pond dry out

1984 – Topographical identification plaque installed by the Greater London Council on The Point for the benefit of sightseers

1986 – Greater London Council abolished. Greenwich and Lewisham take on responsibility for the Heath where it falls within the respective boroughs. The A2 (although not an exact boundary) marked the division between the boroughs for ease of management.

1987 – Greenwich Council's intention to install a public weighbridge on the Heath outside the Blackheath Gate withdrawn after huge public outcry and letters to *The Times*

1987 - Establishment of the Blackheath Advisory Group (later the Blackheath Joint Working Party) to monitor the use and management of the Heath. Membership initially consisted of the Greenwich and Lewisham parks departments and the leading local amenity societies, and was later expanded.

October 1987 – The Great Storm. Many mature trees on the edge of the Heath and near the ponds lost

1990 – *Tidy Blackheath Group* founded by Mrs Margaret Dinkeldein

1994 – Funfairs curtailed because of lasting damage to the Circus Field. Christmas funfair abolished

May 1995 – Heavy lorry ban through Greenwich town centre pushed considerable commercial traffic on to the A2

31 December 1999/1 January 2000 – Spontaneous demonstrations of happiness by local population at midnight to mark the advent of the new Millennium. Huge firework display.

2000 – London Ecology Unit report on *Nature Conservation in Lewisham*, by John Archer and Ian Yarham, includes substantial section on the Heath

2000 – Closure of the original Long Pond Road. This, along with Whitefield Road and parts of Duke Humphrey Road and Mounts Pond Road, reduced to width of foot and cycle paths

2000 – Care of Heath within Lewisham catchment deputed to Glendale Management Co Ltd.

2001 – World Heritage Site Action Plan for Blackheath Gate and adjacent facilities proposed

Summer 2002 – Major subsidence on Blackheath Hill closed the A2 across Blackheath for some months

March 2003 – Heath Keeper's House repaired and occupied

March 2003 – *Blackheath: The next 50 years*. Report on the future of the Heath by town planning consultant Kim Wilkie

July 2003 – First *Race for Life* on Blackheath

East & West Mills by Ralph W. Lucas 1829

18 November 2003 – Restoration of Gibb Memorial Shelter, at south end of Maze Hill

June 2008 – First Bike & Kite Festival

July 2008 – Local sports' clubs: Royal Blackheath Golf, Blackheath Football and the Blackheath Hockey, marked a notional 400th anniversary of sport on the Heath; many participants played in period costume.

August 2009 – Illegal "Climate Camp" on Heath for three days, engendering no mess and no fuss.

2010 – Blackheath wins its first Civic Trust Green Flag award

December 2011 – Lewisham and Greenwich councils adopt a joint Blackheath Events Policy to avoid "culture clash"

24 June 2012 – Blackheath Society marked its 75th anniversary, HM The Queen's Diamond Jubilee and the London Olympic Games with placement of the landmark Hub on the Heath at the old Long Pond Road - Duke Humphrey Road crossing

July-August 2012 – XXXth Modern Olympiad came to London. Equestrian events staged in Greenwich Park. Circus Field on the Heath enclosed for support services and a "logistics compound" for the event.

2012 – Old style lamp posts erected on some of the Heath footpaths partly funded by English Heritage.

2013 – Detailed surveys of flora and fauna at Eliot Pits, Hyde Vale, and Talbot Place by David Notton

28 June 2013 – Unveiled at The Point, memorial stone to RAF Hurricane pilot, Fl. Lt. Richard Reynell, who was killed in action on 7th September 1940, close to this spot.

November 2013 – Blackheath walkers' guide and this Timeline published by the Blackheath Society

----

Aerial view 1990s

The Paragon in the winter of 2012

How You Can Help

In order to achieve its objectives of preserving and enhancing the many attractive features of Blackheath, the Society needs the support of as many members of the community as possible.

Whether or not you live in Blackheath, we hope you will wish to join the Society and give it your support.

Join The Blackheath Society

The annual subscription is a minimum of £20 per household.

Payment by standing order is greatly preferred and completion of a Gift Aid declaration will help the Society further.

Life Membership is also available.

Contact Us

For any other queries, please contact the Secretary for more information about the Society.
The office is normally open from
9am-2pm Monday to Thursday.

Our telephone number is **020 8297 1937**
email us: **office@blackheath.org**
Facebook: **BlackheathSociety**
Twitter: **@BlackheathSoc**
www.blackheath.org

The Blackheath Society
The Old Bakehouse
11 Blackheath Village
London SE3 9LA

The Blackheath Society is a Registered Charity. Number 259843.

Back cover photograph of Race for Life, 2013 by Roger Marshall